OPEN ROAD

Pearson Education ESL
Canadian Titles and Authors

Canadian Stories by Eleanor Adamowski

The Longman Picture Dictionary, Canadian ed., by Julie Ashworth & John Clark

Reading for the Write Reasons: English Reading and Writing for Advanced ESL Students by Donna Aziz-Canuel, Lynne Gaetz & Richard Pawsey

Amazing! News Interviews & Conversations by Susan Bates

Amazing! Canadian Newspaper Stories by Susan Bates

Amazing 2! News Interviews & Conversations by Susan Bates

Amazing 2! Canadian Newspaper Stories by Susan Bates

Canadian Concepts, 2nd ed., Books 1-6 by Lynda Berish & Sandra Thibaudeau

English Fast Forward 1, 2nd ed., by Lynda Berish & Sandra Thibaudeau

English Fast Forward 2, 2nd ed., by Lynda Berish & Sandra Thibaudeau

English Fast Forward 3, 2nd ed., by Lynda Berish & Sandra Thibaudeau

Grammar Connections, Books 1, 2 & 3, by Lynda Berish & Sandra Thibaudeau

On Target by Keith L. Boeckner & Joan Polfuss Boeckner

On Target Too by Keith L. Boeckner & Joan Polfuss Boeckner

Target Practice by Keith L. Boeckner & Joan Polfuss Boeckner

Classics Canada: Authentic Readings for ESL Students, Books 1-4, by Patricia Brock & Brian John Busby

Coming to Canada: Authentic Reading for ESL Students by Patricia Brock & Brian John Busby

Contemporary Canada: Authentic Readings for ESL Students by Patricia Brock & Brian John Busby

Being Canadian: Language for Citizenship by Judy Cameron & Tracey M. Derwing

Focus 2: Academic Listening and Speaking Skills by Ranka Curcin, Mary Koumoulas, & Sonia Fiorucci-Nicholls

Focus 2: Academic Reading Skills by Ranka Curcin, Mary Koumoulas, & Sonia Fiorucci-Nicholls

Focus 2: Academic Writing Skills by Ranka Curcin, Mary Koumoulas, & Sonia Fiorucci-Nicholls

Writing for Success: Preparing for Business, Technology, Trades and Career Programs by Dale Fitzpatrick & Kathleen Center Vance

All Right! A Guide to Correct English by Paul Fournier

Blueprints: A Guide to Correct Writing by Paul Fournier

English on Demand, 2nd ed., by Paul Fournier

English on Line, 2nd ed., by Paul Fournier

English on Purpose, 2nd ed., by Paul Fournier

This Side Up by Paul Fournier

This Way Out by Paul Fournier

Before Brass Tacks: Basic Grammar by Lynne Gaetz

Before Brass Tacks: Basic Skills in English by Lynne Gaetz

Brass Ring 1: Basic English for Career-Related Communication by Lynne Gaetz

Brass Ring 1: Basic Grammar Review by Lynne Gaetz

Brass Ring 2: English for Career-Related Communication by Lynne Gaetz

Brass Ring 2: Grammar Review by Lynne Gaetz

Brass Tacks Grammar by Lynne Gaetz

Brass Tacks: Integrated Skills in English by Lynne Gaetz

Open Book English Skills by Lynne Gaetz

Open Book Grammar by Lynne Gaetz

Open Road English Skills by Lynne Gaetz

Open Road Grammar by Lynne Gaetz

Open Window English Skills by Lynne Gaetz

Open Window Grammar by Lynne Gaetz

Bridge to Fluency by Elizabeth Gatbonton

Links: ESL Writing and Editing by Carolyn Greene & Claudia Rock

A Beginning Look at Canada, 2nd ed., by Anne-Marie Kaskens

A Canadian Conversation Book: English in Everyday Life, 2nd ed., Book 1, by Tina Kasloff Carver, Sandra Douglas Fotinos & Clarice Cooper

Writing for Results: Academic and Professional Writing Tasks by H. M. McGarell & P. Brillinger

Reading Matters: A Selection of Canadian Writing by Jane Merivale

Word-by-Word Beginning Workbook, Canadian ed., by Steven Molinsky & Bill Bliss

Word-by-Word Intermediate Workbook, Canadian ed. by Steven Molinsky & Bill Bliss

Word-by-Word Picture Dictionary, Canadian ed. by Steven Molinsky & Bill Bliss

Take Charge: Using Everyday Canadian English by Lucia Pietrusiak Engkent

Take Part: Speaking Canadian English, 2nd ed., by Lucia Pietrusiak Engkent & Karen P. Bardy

Technically Speaking…: Writing, Reading and Listening, English at Work by Susan Quirk Drolet & Ann Farrell Séguin

Style and Substance: A Multimedia Approach to Literature and Composition by Claudia Rock & Suneeti Phadke

Read on Canada by Paul Sharples & Judith Clark

Getting it Together, Books 1 & 2, by Véra Téophil Naber

A Grammar Manual, Volumes A & B, by Véra Téophil Naber & Savitsa Sévigny

Advanced Half-Hour Helper: Puzzles and Activities for ESL Students by Joan Roberta White

Half-Hour Helper: Puzzles and Activities for ESL Students by Joan Roberta White

Making the Grade: An Interactive Course in English for Academic Purposes by David Wood

OPEN ROAD

ENGLISH SKILLS

Lynne Gaetz

Vancouver Community College
College Prep English

PEARSON Longman ESL
DISTRIBUTED IN CANADA BY ERPI

5757, RUE CYPIHOT, SAINT-LAURENT (QUÉBEC) H4S 1R3
TÉLÉPHONE : (514) 334-2690 TÉLÉCOPIEUR : (514) 334-4720
COURRIEL : erpidlm@erpi.com www.erpi.com

Acknowledgements

I would like to express sincere thanks to:
- Claudia Rock and Joyce Rappaport for their invaluable editing.
- Jean-Pierre Albert, Julie Champoux, and the team at diabolo-menthe.
- All of my colleagues at Collège Lionel-Groulx. They are truly a comfortable and inspiring group of people to work with.
- Everyone who agreed to be interviewed for the book.
- My colleagues throughout the province who kindly provided feedback:
  Ann Kelly, Cégep Abitimi-Témiscamingue
  Geraldine Arbach, Collège de l'outaouais
  Peggy Swan Bérubé, Institut Maritime du Québec
  Barbara Fraser, Collège Ahuntsic
  Hugh Bourgoyne, Cégep de St-Jérôme
  Deborah Albert, UVCS, English Language Centre, Continuing Studies, BC

Finally, I would like to extend special thanks to my husband and children.

Project Editor:
Joyce Rappaport

Book design and page layout:
diabolo-menthe

© 2002 Longman, Published and distributed by
ÉDITIONS DU RENOUVEAU PÉDAGOGIQUE INC.

All rights reserved.

This book is explicitly excluded from any photocopy agreements in existence. Photocopying of any part of *Open Road English Skills* is illegal without prior written permission from the publisher.

Registration of copyright: 1st quarter 2002
Bibliothèque nationale du Québec
National Library of Canada
Printed in Canada

ISBN 2-7613-1313-5
567890 II 0987654
131313 CD   OF2-10

Credits

The following authors, publishers, and photographers have generously given permission to reproduce copyright material.

WRITING THE ACADEMIC ESSAY REFERENCE SECTION. "Marriage Mythology" by Tara Blanc. Reproduced by permission of the author. Text originally appeared in *ASU Research Magazine*.

CHAPTER 1. "How Travel Changed My Life" by Arthur Frommer. Arthur Frommer's Budget Travel Online http://www.frommers.com/ Reprinted with permission. Photograph of Train in India courtesy of Manuel Djamdjian / Gamma / PONOPRESSE.

CHAPTER 2. "The Ghost Next Door" by Bertram Rothschild. Reproduced by permission of the author. "The Night the Martians Attacked" by Lee Krystek. Reprinted with permission of the author. Some items in the "Moments in Time" speaking activity originally appeared in the CBC TV *News in Review Resource Guide* (Mar. 1992). Reprinted with permission. Photograph of Orson Welles courtesy of Shooting Star / PONOPRESSE.

CHAPTER 3. "When Our Sports Idols Go on Trial" by Lisa Fitterman. Reprinted with permission of *The Gazette* (Montreal) and Lisa Fitterman. "Man, You're a Great Player" from Laughing with Lautens, copyright 1964 by Gary Lautens. Reprinted with permission of Jacqueline Lautens. Photograph of Dave Hilton courtesy of Michel Ponomareff / PONOPRESSE. Photograph of Hockey fight courtesy of Michel Ponomareff / PONOPRESSE.

CHAPTER 4. Question 5 from the "Columbus: Hero or Villain" listening exercise first appeared in the CBC's *News in Review Resource Guide*, Nov. 1992, p. 45. Reprinted by permission. "Racism is panicky reaction to change" by Gwynn Dyer, *Montreal Gazette*, 26 August 2000. Reprinted by permission of the author. "P is for Prejudice" by Allen Abel. Abridged version. Reproduced by permission of the author. "Conscience" by Italo Calvino. Reprinted by permission of The Wylie Agency.

CHAPTER 5. "Next Door", from *Welcome to the Monkey House* by Kurt Vonnegut, Jr, copyright 1961 by Kurt Vonnegut Jr. Used by permission of Dell Publishing, a division of Random House.

CHAPTER 6. "The Real Alternative" by Veena Thomas. Reprinted by permission of the author. Photograph of Sid Vicious and Nancy courtesy of London Features / PONOPRESSE. Photograph of Louise Brooks courtesy of Sipa Press / PONOPRESSE. Photograph of Scott Fitzgerald and Zelda courtesy of Topham / PONOPRESSE

CHAPTER 7. "Marriage—Many-Splendored, Sometimes Splintered Thing" by Daniel Wayne Matthews. Reprinted by permission of the author. "The Chaser" by John Collier. Originally published in *The New Yorker*. Reprinted by permission of Harold Matson, Agent. Copyright © 1940 by John Collier.

Table of Contents

OPEN ROAD Integrated Skills in English

Writing: The Academic Essay

The Topic Sentence	2
Paragraph Unity and Form	3
Essay Structure	4
The Thesis Statement	5
Supporting the Thesis Statement	6
The Introduction	8
The Conclusion	11
Transitions Between Paragraphs	13

CHAPTER 1 — Village of Idiots

WARM UP	Proverbs and Quotations	15
READING TIP	Using Context Clues	16
Reading 1.1	"How Travel Changed My Life" by Arthur Frommer	17
WATCHING	Village of Idiots (NFB)	20
LISTENING	Travel Stories from Syria	22
Reading 1.2	"The Passenger" by Julie Nehme	23
WRITING	Using Descriptive Language	26
SPEAKING	Life Experience	27

CHAPTER 2 — Skeptical Minds

WARM UP	Fact or Fantasy?	29
WATCHING	JFK: What's Fact, What's Not? (CBC)	30
SPEAKING	Moments in Time	32
READING TIP	Determine Bias	34
Reading 2.1	"The Ghost in My House" by Bertram Rothschild	36
Reading 2.2	"The Mesmerizer" by Mark Twain	39
Reading 2.3	"The Night the Martians Attacked" by Lee Krystek	43
LISTENING	Orson Welles	46
SPEAKING	Create a Radio Play	47
WRITING	Essay Topics	48

CHAPTER 3 — The Greatest Players

WARM UP	Admirable Individuals	49
Reading 3.1	"When Our Sports Idols Go On Trial" by Lisa Fitterman	50
SPEAKING	Are they Heroes?	53
WATCHING	The Hero Among Us (CBC)	54
READING TIP	Recognizing Irony	56
Reading 3.2	"The Greatest Player" by Gary Lautens	57
LISTENING	Murder on Ice	60
WRITING	Essay Topics	61

© Longman

CHAPTER 4 Conscience

WARM UP	Cultural Connections	62
WATCHING	Columbus, Hero or Villain	62
READING TIP	Determine the Author's Purpose	63
	Pair Reading Activity	64
	Reading 4.1 "Racism's Source" by Gwynne Dyer	64
	Reading 4.2 "P is for Prejudice" by Allen Abel	67
LISTENING	Pakistan	71
SPEAKING	Developing Strong Arguments	72
SPEAKING ACTIVITY	The Corporal Hanes Case	73
	Debate or Present a Controversial Issue	75
	Reading 4.3 "Conscience" by Italo Calvino	76
WRITING	Essay Topics	78

CHAPTER 5 Innocence

WARM UP	Team Discussions	79
	Reading 5.1 "Childhood: A Time of Innocence?" by Adele Berridge	82
READING TIP	Think about the Story (plot)	85
	Reading 5.2 "Next Door" by Kurt Vonnegut Jr.	86
SPEAKING	How to Raise a Well-Adjusted Child	96
WRITING	Essay Topics	96

CHAPTER 6 Initiation

WARM UP	Initiation Rituals	97
SPEAKING	Youth Culture	97
	Reading 6.1 "The Real Alternative" by Veena Thomas	98
READING TIP	Think about the Setting and Characters	100
	Reading 6.2 "Bernice Bobs Her Hair" by F. Scott Fitzgerald	102
LISTENING	Scott and Zelda	122
WRITING TIP	Writing about Fiction	123
WRITING	Essay Topics	124

CHAPTER 7 Love

WARM UP	Relationship Survey	126
	Reading 7.1 "Marriage Myths" by Daniel Wayne Matthews	127
LISTENING	Love	130
READING TIP	Making Inferences	131
	Reading 7.2 "The Chaser" by John Collier	133
READING TIP	Think about the Theme (meaning)	137
WRITING	Essay Topics	138

Appendices

1	How to do Oral Presentations	139
2	Speaking Presentation Topic – Classic Movie Analysis	140
3	Classic Movie Suggestions	142
4	Twenty Controversial Issues	144

Introduction

Essays come in a variety of shapes and sizes. The term *essay* can encompass everything from the humour column in Saturday's paper to the serious condemnation of capitalism found in a political pamphlet. Essays can, among other things, inform us, persuade us to see things differently, tell us a story, describe an event, make us laugh, or give us factual information.

Unlike the short story, the essay deals with subject matter that is, for the most part, nonfiction. While the short story is developed in the imagination of the writer, the essay is born in reality.

This book includes essays and short stories. The theme of the **Open Road** permeates this book. Stories deal with adventure, experience, and discovery. You will also be asked to consider the validity of common beliefs.

Enjoy the open road!

To the Teacher

Directed at high-intermediate to advanced students of English as a second language, **Open Road** is a comprehensive integrated-skills text.

Seven chapters contain a variety of reading styles including informative, persuasive and narrative essays, interviews, and short stories by internationally acclaimed authors. Throughout the book students are asked to critically evaluate what they read.

Teachers who want to teach basic literary analysis at this level have the opportunity to do so, and there are explanations about plot, character, setting and theme as well as references to some literary devices such as irony and personification. For those who want to avoid formal literary analysis, the four short stories could be approached simply as another reading format with a focus on what happened, who it happened to, and what it all means.

The Reference Section, Writing the Academic Essay, contains detailed examinations of topic sentences, paragraphs, thesis statements, supporting arguments and conclusions as well as transitions between paragraphs. You can teach elements of academic writing at any point in the course, or you could ask students to review the reference section independently.

Writing The Academic Essay

In this course you will learn to write an academic essay. This section explains the parts of the essay and gives you some practice in essay writing.

The Paragraph

THE TOPIC SENTENCE

Essays are made up of paragraphs, and each paragraph focuses on one main idea. In a paragraph, the point that you are trying to make should be clearly evident in an interesting **topic sentence**. Everything else in the paragraph should be a detail that supports your topic sentence.

- A good topic sentence should not be too general or too specific.

    Life is difficult. (Too general)
    Twenty percent of adults feel stressed. (Too specific)

- A good topic sentence should express both the subject of the paragraph and a central point about that subject.

    Traveling teaches us that people are basically alike.
       subject   central point about the subject

Writing Exercise 1 – Write Topic Sentences

Write a topic sentence for the following paragraph. Remember that your sentence must make a central point about the topic and must unify the paragraph.

Topic sentence: _____

_____

> For example, a recent survey of married couples conducted by Ballit suggests that women with full-time jobs spend about 18 hours per week on housework whereas men spend only seven. Some things have changed since the 1950s; men cook and wash dishes more often than they did in the past. However, only seven percent of men surveyed do their own laundry, and just three percent clean the toilet on a regular basis. It is no surprise, then, to discover that two thirds of women surveyed feel stressed and overworked.

PARAGRAPH UNITY

A good topic sentence unifies the paragraph. The topic sentence should be general enough that all of the details and examples in the paragraph relate back to it. Don't include facts in your paragraph that have nothing to do with the topic sentence.

Writing Exercise 2 – Analyze a Paragraph

Read the following paragraph and identify the topic sentence. Then cross out any sentences that are not related to the topic sentence. (Remember, the topic sentence doesn't have to be the first sentence of a paragraph.)

> Anaïs Nin, one of the most famous diary-writers of all time, has claimed that keeping a diary was her way of making everyday life feel as exciting as fiction. If you want to be a writer, diary keeping is an ideal way to exercise your craft. Because diary writing is not meant for an audience, it can free your creativity. Daily writing is like practicing the scales on a piano: you express yourself in your given art without worrying about the final product. However, some writers are tormented and have unhealthy lifestyles. William Burroughs had a drug habit. Other writers, such as Jack Kerouac and F. Scott Fitzgerald, were alcoholics. The best writers practice their craft every day. According to Henry Miller, "to write each day is the thing. Not to turn out masterpieces."

PARAGRAPH FORM – SUPPORTING THE TOPIC SENTENCE

Like longer essays, paragraphs have an internal form. They contain the following:

- A topic sentence that expresses the main idea of the paragraph.
- Other sentences that reinforce the main idea. The other sentences may provide examples, facts, statistics, or anecdotal evidence.
- A concluding sentence that sums up the main point or expresses another notion about the topic.

Writing Exercise 3 – Analyze a Paragraph

Read the following paragraph and then answer the questions that follow.

> When children are involved, divorce is never painless. To minimize the problems associated with divorce, parents need to maintain a stable environment for their children. For example, any fighting over finances or child visitation should not occur in front of the children. Also, parents should try to live near each other so that the child has easy access to both parents. To further stabilize the child's life after a divorce, many parents now opt for the "family home." The kids don't have to change houses to visit each parent; instead, the parents take turns living in the family home. If parents just remember to put children first, then the effects of divorce on the children can be minimized.

1 Highlight the topic sentence.

2 How is the topic sentence supported? In point form, list the three supporting ideas.

_____

_____

_____

3 Highlight the concluding statement.

The Essay

> **ESSAY STRUCTURE**
>
> ### The Introduction
> A good introduction has two main characteristics:
> - It captures the attention of the reader.
> - The thesis, or main subject of the essay, should be mentioned in the introduction.
>
> A *thesis statement* is a general opinion statement. The arguments in the body of the essay should provide the supporting reasons for the thesis statement.
>
> ### The Body Paragraphs
> The body paragraphs should back up the thesis statement with clear reasons.
> - Remember that each body paragraph should focus on one central idea. This idea is stated in the paragraph's *topic sentence*.
> - The paragraph should then be developed with *supporting facts and examples*. The facts and examples should be directly related to the topic sentence (focus sentence) of the paragraph.
>
> ### The Conclusion
> The concluding paragraph, which brings the essay to a satisfying end, can have the following form.
> - The main points are restated but not repeated.
> - The conclusion could end with a prediction, suggestion, quotation, or solution.
>
> Do not introduce a contradictory point, and do not end your text with a question.

Writing Exercise 4 – Identify Essay Elements

Look at the following essay. Using a highlighter pen, identify the following parts of the essay:

1. Introduction: Highlight the thesis statement.
2. Body: Highlight the topic sentences for two body paragraphs.
3. Conclusion: Highlight words or phrases that restate some main arguments.

Marriage Mythology

by Tara Blanc

Introduction — When it comes to marriage, we expect the fairy tale. Raised on *Cinderella* and *Ozzie and Harriet*, we're convinced that marriage will solve all of our problems, our partner will meet all of our needs, and that we'll live happily ever after. But a great many of us don't get the happily-ever-after part; we get divorced. So where did we go wrong? Mary Laner, a professor of sociology at Arizona State University, lays at least part of the blame for high divorce rates on unrealistic expectations.

Body 1 — The move away from tribal or village economies into a mass society has fostered our sense of individualism, and this has had an impact on our expectations. "When you break away from those kinds of economies and get into more depersonalized societies, you get individualistic thinking," Laner says. "We tend to think 'when I marry, this is what I want; these are the expectations I have for getting married.' More collective thinking would be: 'when I marry, it will be good for my village.'"

Body 2 — "Ultimately, you get expressions like 'I'm not marrying her family, I'm marrying her,'" she adds. "But, of course, you *are* marrying her family and she's marrying yours." We expect one person to meet an impossible volume of needs, yet we dismiss the baggage that our spouse necessarily brings to the relationship. We expect our mate to take care of us, raise the children, pursue a career and let us pursue ours, fix the plumbing, cook the meals, keep the house clean and, of course, be a caring, considerate friend and lover. But we don't expect to have problems with in-laws.

Conclusion — Laner doesn't foresee that our high expectations will change. "We don't live in the kind of society where families or tribes or villages want to tie themselves to one another through the marriage bond," she says. "If anything, we'll have more individualism and more failed expectations."

The Thesis Statement

The thesis statement is a statement of opinion and it identifies the subject of the essay. In reports or research papers it is useful to let the reader know immediately what your arguments are going to be. However, in opinion essay writing, this removes the punch from subsequent paragraphs. Therefore, in opinion essays, simply state your opinion and leave your main points for the body of the essay.

Thesis statement

Marriage has lost its importance for many young people in our society.

subject | your opinion about the subject

THESIS STATEMENT PROBLEMS

- Your thesis statement should focus on one central idea. Do not try to argue too many points or your essay will lack unity.
  There are good and bad things about zoos.
  There is no central focus.

- Your thesis statement should express an opinion, not a fact.
  I am going to talk about primates.
  This is not a thesis statement! No opinion is expressed.

- Your thesis statement should be in statement form and not in question form.
  How can we protect endangered species?
  This is not a thesis statement. It is a question.

- Phrases like "I believe" or "I am going to talk about" are unnecessary and redundant. Do not include them in your thesis statement.

A good thesis statement is a focused statement of opinion.
Although zoos keep some endangered species from extinction, primates should not be kept in captivity.

Writing Exercise 5 – Analyze Thesis Statements

Most of the following thesis statements are weak. Analyze and edit them. Which thesis statement is best? What is wrong with the others?

1. Money.

2. I am going to talk about money.

3. Why do we need money?

4. I think that money will not solve our problems.

5. I am going to discuss how a lot of money can cause more problems than it solves because it makes people feel useless, paranoid, and frightened.

6. Although many people think that money will solve their problems, a cash windfall often causes more problems than it solves.

Supporting the Thesis Statement

Thesis statements must be supported with clear reasons. Each reason becomes the focus of a supporting paragraph.

Supporting paragraphs can include anecdotes, statistics, quotations, or any other relevant supporting material.

THESIS STATEMENT	SUPPORTING ARGUMENTS
Although many people think money will solve their problems, a cash windfall often causes more problems than it solves.	• With nothing to work for, the newly rich often feel useless. • Lottery winners and inheritors generally feel guilty about their wealth. • When money enters the picture, the newly rich often become a little paranoid because they suspect that others want to take advantage of them.

Writing Exercise 6 – Write Thesis Statements and Topic Sentences

Create an interesting thesis statement for one of the following topics. Then write three topic sentences that support your thesis statement.

| war | beauty | health | fame | family | heroism |

Thesis statement: _____

_____

Supporting arguments (in point form)

  Topic Sentence 1: _____

  Topic Sentence 2: _____

  Topic Sentence 3: _____

Writing Exercise 7 – Write Thesis Statements and Topic Sentences

Read the following essay. After you have finished reading, do the following:

1. Create an effective thesis (opinion) statement. The thesis statement sums up the point of the entire essay.

2. At the beginning of each body paragraph, write topic sentences. The topic sentence should sum up the main point of the paragraph in an interesting way.

Travel Tips

Introduction

Danger has always been synonymous with travel. In past centuries, pirates on the high seas attacked passing ships. Land travelers weren't much safer; bandits could attack their covered carriages. Even trains weren't safe; in 1877 the masked outlaw Sam Bass held up a train in Nebraska and robbed the passengers. Today, with modern communication and with high-speed trains and planes, travel is quick and relatively risk-free. Nonetheless, there are still certain hazards inherent in traveling.

→

Thesis statement: _____
_____

Body 1 Topic sentence: _____
_____

If you walk around at night carrying a backpack, you might as well write "I'm a naïve tourist" on your forehead. Nineteen-year-old Jim Lee had an unfortunate incident when he arrived in Amsterdam at 11 pm. He wandered around for hours trying to find a cheap youth hostel. When he went into a particularly quiet street, a trio of men surrounded him and took his backpack and sneakers.

Body 2 Topic sentence: _____
_____

You could wear a money belt. One innovative solution is to sew long, extended pockets on the insides of your pants; you could keep your checks and passport there. In a small, easily accessible purse or wallet, keep small amounts of local currency for your daily spending.

Body 3 Topic sentence: _____
_____

For example, thieves might work in teams of two or three. One distracts you; he could make conversation with you. Another reaches into your pack or pocket, and a third keeps a watch out for police. Don't forget that for some people, theft is much more than a hobby: it is a profession.

Conclusion Although robberies can happen, it is unlikely that someone will physically hurt you. If you take risks, if you are careless with your money and passports, or if you underestimate thieves, you may get robbed. Of course, if you are careful, you should have a perfectly safe and exciting trip.

The Introduction

INTRODUCTION STYLES

There are many common introduction styles. Look at the following four introductions. The thesis statements are highlighted.

- **Begin with an anecdote or description.**

  Dorothy Duke, the tobacco heiress, was filthy rich but she was renowned as an unhappy woman. She spent her waning years as a recluse. She had no friends or family at her bedside during her final hours; indeed, some speculate that her own staff hastened her demise. In Dorothy's case, money did not buy her happiness or peace of mind. **Although many people feel that money will solve their problems, too much money may cause more problems than it solves.**

- **Describe the opposite position.** Then disagree with that position.

  Life would be great if you just won the lottery. There would be no work-related stress. You could stay home, sit by the pool, or play a game of golf. With a lot of money, you wouldn't worry about your retirement: you could retire now! That nice house by the beach could be yours. It sounds great, right!? But living a life of ease may not be so fantastic after all. **Money does not necessarily lead to happiness.**

- **Begin with historical information.**

  In the past, civilizations bartered with items. A cow could be traded for a small plot of land. Later, silver and gold were formed into coins. Since the coins translated into more goods or more land, they were coveted. Today, we are a money-obsessed nation. Everybody wants the dream house, the nice car, and the vacation by a beach. **However, if you want to be truly happy, the pursuit of money should not guide your life.**

- **Begin with general background information.**

  You can't deny that we need money to function in this society. Money pays our rent, buys us food and clothing, and pays for our transportation. It is possible to have too little money to survive. Just ask any homeless person. But it is also possible to have too much money. **Although many people feel that money will solve their problems, too much money may cause more problems than it solves.**

AVOID THE FOLLOWING PROBLEMS IN YOUR INTRODUCTION

1. *I'm going to talk about…*

   Do not begin an essay this way.

2. *Should children watch television? I don't think so.*

   It is not a good idea to ask and answer questions in your introduction.

3. *When people suddenly get a lot of money, they think that their life will get better, but it often gets worse because the newly rich feel guilty, they get bored, and then they usually feel as unhappy as they did before they got the windfall.*

   Avoid giving away all of your arguments in the introduction. Simply state your point of view in an interesting way, and save your supporting arguments for the body of your essay.*

* Some writing manuals disagree with this point. If your teacher wants you to present your main arguments in the introduction, then you should do it.

Writing Exercise 8 – Analyze Introductions

Read the following introductions. In each introduction, highlight the thesis statement.

At the bottom of each introduction, indicate which type of opening sentence is used, and also indicate which style is used: anecdote, description, or background information.

A	B
"Your father and I are getting a divorce." To eight-year-old Simon Dirk, these words struck terror. His world disintegrated. Suddenly, home was no longer a safe place. His parents talked of two bedrooms, of visitation rights, of the need to remember that everything would be okay. The problem was, to Simon everything was definitely not okay. **Divorce may seem like the best solution for parents, but it can have a huge impact on children.**	For every marriage that succeeds, there is another one that fails. This harsh statistic reflects a social system that is in rapid transformation. A mere fifty years ago divorce was taboo; only Hollywood types openly did it. For the rest of the population, divorce was seen as an immoral act. People often remained in cold or even abusive relationships because divorce was not a viable solution. **Luckily, the world has changed and one can leave a loveless marriage, thus improving both the parents' and the child's lives.**
Circle the answers that best describe this introduction. **Introductory sentence:** a) controversial statement b) quotation c) statistic **Introduction style:** a) anecdote c) historical b) opposite view d) general background	Circle the answers that best describe this introduction. **Introductory sentence:** a) controversial statement b) quotation c) statistic **Introduction style:** a) anecdote c) historical b) opposite view d) general background

Writing Exercise 9 – Write Three Introductions

Choose **one** of the following thesis statements. Then write three introductions using three different introduction styles. Use the same thesis statement in each introduction.

1. *It is important to know more than one language.*
2. *Famous musicians generally make poor (or good) role models.*
3. *Our society is (or is not) obsessed with beauty.*
4. *There are several reasons that nations enter wars.*
5. Use the thesis statement that you created for Writing Exercise 6.
6. Your choice.

Choose any three of the following styles. You can:

- tell an anecdote
- describe the opposite position and then disagree with that position
- give historical information about the topic
- give general background information about the topic

Highlight the thesis statement in each introduction.

The Conclusion

Your conclusion should do three things:
- restate the thesis.
- summarize your main points.
- make an interesting closing statement. You could end with a suggestion, prediction, or quotation.

Do not introduce new or contradictory information in the conclusion.

Do not always end with a rhetorical question. (A rhetorical question is a question that won't be answered. Example: *When will people learn to appreciate what they've got?*)

Writing Exercise 10 – Write an Introduction and Conclusion

On a separate sheet of paper, write an introduction and conclusion for the following essay.
- First, read the body of the essay. Highlight the topic sentence in each paragraph. Ask yourself what the central point of the essay is.
- Once you have determined the central point of the essay, you can plan your thesis statement.
- Write a compelling introduction and highlight your thesis statement. Choose one of the introduction styles that you learned in this unit.
- Write a conclusion. Restate the main points. Make an interesting closing statement.

→ **Write an Introduction**

First, the health of children has changed since the introduction of television. Now that TVs are an important part of everybody's home, too many children spend their free time sitting in front of the set. Ben Tyler, a 10-year-old Montrealer, states that he watches between five and seven hours of television each day. "I can watch whatever I want," he says proudly. But Ben is also overweight and suffers from asthma. His mother sees no connection between his excessive TV watching and his health problems.

Furthermore, family communication suffers when a television is present. The TV is on while we eat dinner, the TV amuses us in the evening, and the TV replaces the bedtime story. Jonathan, a sixteen-year old college student, claims that he hasn't really talked to his parents for years. "We have two-minute conversations. When they get home from work, they put the TV on and everybody watches it. We have a TV in the kitchen and we watch *Friends* reruns every day. It's fun and I like it, but I guess I don't know about my parents' lives and they don't know about my life."

Too often, when people do communicate, their discussions revolve around television shows. Thirty-year-old William and his friend Jay love nothing more than to reminisce about their favorite programs. "I know the theme songs for about fifteen television shows," William says. When asked his opinion about the latest political crisis, Jay says, "The only politics I care about are on *The West Wing*."

→ **Write a Conclusion**

Writing Exercise 11 – Identify Essay Problems

Look at the following parts of the essay. What structural problems exist? How can the essay be improved?

The Introduction

How can children be protected? Should they be protected from the dark sides of life? I don't think so. In my essay, I'm going to talk about how children should not be overprotected.

1 What are some problems with this introduction?
_____
_____

2 How could this introduction be improved?
_____
_____

The Body

Children have to be told about bad things in the world. For example, you should warn your children about the dangers of cigarette smoking. You should tell them about the damage that nicotine does to human lungs. If you don't properly warn your children, they may start to smoke as soon as they see their friends smoking. So remember that children should not be overprotected, and you must let them face the dark sides of life.

3 Is this supporting argument logical? _____

4 Does it contain supporting facts and examples? _____

5 What would make a better supporting argument? Think of some ideas.
_____
_____
_____
_____

The Conclusion

So remember that you must let children make mistakes and learn from them. Then children will be able to face difficult moments when they grow up. But can you really overprotect a child?

6 What is wrong with this conclusion? _____
_____

7 What would make a more effective closing sentence? _____
_____

Transitions Between Paragraphs

If you were to ride on a train and pieces of the track were missing, you would be in for a very bumpy ride. When you write an essay, there must be transitional phrases between paragraphs to ensure that the reader has a smooth ride through your arguments. In order to guide the reader from one idea to the next, or from one paragraph to the next, there are some methods that can be employed.

1) Briefly refer to the previous argument, and link it to your current argument. Examine the following example.

Thesis statement: *A cash windfall may cause more problems than it solves.*
- Paragraph 1 topic sentence: *The newly rich often lose their desire to become productive citizens, and they end up feeling useless.*
- Paragraph 2 topic sentence – with transition: <u>*Many heirs and lottery winners feel useless;* *morever, they also tend to feel guilty about their wealth.*</u>
In this sentence the reader is briefly reminded of the previous point (*the newly rich feel useless*) and then introduced to the next point (*The newly rich feel guilty*).

2) With a transitional word or phrase, lead the reader to your next idea.
<u>*Furthermore*</u>, *the newly rich often feel guilty about their wealth.*

TRANSITIONAL WORDS AND PHRASES

These transitional words and expressions help the reader follow the logic of a text.

CHRONOLOGY (sequence of ideas)	ADDITIONAL ARGUMENT	CONCLUDING EXPRESSIONS	CONTRASTING IDEAS
first to begin with in the first place second third finally	furthermore moreover additionally besides also	therefore thus finally to conclude in conclusion in short to sum up on the whole	on the one hand on the other hand on the contrary although even though whereas in spite of however nevertheless

EMPHASIS		ILLUSTRATION / EXAMPLE	CAUSE AND EFFECT
indeed in fact surely certainly	clearly definitely undoubtedly especially	for example to illustrate for instance namely that is	otherwise because since (meaning "because") due to until as soon as

Writing Exercise 12 – Transitional Phrases

To ensure that you understand the following, write a definition, example, or translation after each expression.

although _____

even though _____

as long as _____

as soon as _____

besides _____

despite _____

furthermore _____

however _____

in spite of _____

meanwhile _____

moreover _____

nevertheless _____

otherwise _____

therefore _____

thus _____

undoubtedly _____

whereas _____

CHAPTER 1 Village of Idiots

Afoot and light-hearted I take to the open road,
Healthy, free, the world before me.
—Walt Whitman, *Song of the Open Road*

Our lives are an adventure, much like a road to be traveled. In this chapter, Arthur Frommer writes about lessons that he learned while traveling. You will be asked to reflect on your own life experiences.

Proverbs and Quotations

A proverb is a popular saying that expresses a basic truth about life. It often offers advice or a warning. Read the following proverbs. If any proverb or quotation is unclear, discuss it with your classmates and restate it in your own words.

EXAMPLE: Every cloud has a silver lining.
Something good can come out of a bad situation.

- The squeaky wheel gets the grease. (Unknown origin)

- Forever is composed of nows. (Emily Dickinson)

- Don't cross a bridge until you come to it. (English proverb)

- Everyone must row with the oars he has. (English proverb)

- Advice when most needed is least heeded. (English proverb)

- It's better to wear out shoes than sheets. (Scottish proverb)

- Half a loaf is better than none. (English proverb)

- The journey is the reward. (Tao saying)

- It's better to light a candle than to curse the darkness. (Chinese proverb)

- He that plants thorns must never expect to gather roses. (English proverb)

- Let sleeping dogs lie. (English proverb)

- Water which is too pure has no fish. (Ts'ai Ken T'an)

- Nothing dries sooner than tears. (Latin proverb)

- The gem cannot be polished without friction, nor man perfected without trials. (Chinese proverb)

- You cannot unscramble eggs. (North American proverb)

- An eye for an eye leads to a world of the blind. (Mahatma Gandhi)

- Every man I meet is in some way my superior. (Ralph Waldo Emerson)

- Those who cannot remember the past are condemned to repeat it. (George Santayana)

Reading Tip: Using Context Clues

The meaning of many words and expressions can be guessed at when you look at the context in which the word is being used. Use the following strategy when you see an unfamiliar word:

1. **Look at the word.**

   Is the word a noun? Verb? Adjective? Sometimes it is easier to guess the word's meaning when you know how the word functions in the sentence.

2. Look at surrounding words.

Look at the sentence in which the word appears and try to find a relation between the difficult word and the words that surround it. Maybe there is a synonym (word that means the same thing) or antonym (word that means the opposite). Maybe other words in the sentence help define the word.

3. Look at surrounding sentences.

Sometimes the meaning of a difficult word can be guessed by looking at the sentences, paragraphs, and punctuation surrounding the word. When you use logic, the meaning becomes clear.

In most cases, you can guess the meaning of a new word by combining your own knowledge of the topic with the information in the words and phrases surrounding the difficult word.

For example, can you define the word **heed**? _____

Can you define **yearn**? _____

Perhaps you aren't quite sure. Looking at the words in context makes it much easier to guess the definition of the words.

*Travel makes it impossible to pay no **heed** to the sufferings of others, simply because they are far away; it erases distance, and makes you a more sensitive citizen of the world, **yearning** for peace everywhere.*

Now write your own definition or translation of the following words.

heed _____   yearn _____

READING 1.1

The international travel writer, Arthur Frommer, has written extensively about his experiences. In the following text, Frommer explains what traveling has taught him.

How Travel Changed My Life

by Arthur Frommer

1. To nearly a hundred countries, for millions and millions of miles, I've traveled for more than 40 years. And I am a different person because of it. On every trip to everywhere, in unfamiliar surroundings, among new and different people, your consciousness changes and you develop new beliefs — like these:

2. **We are all alike:** I am in the dark, dung hut of a Maasai family in southern Africa. Through an interpreter, the woman of the house tells me that she hopes to learn to read. And why? So she can study a handbook on properly raising children. I am sitting cross-legged on a tatami mat in the apartment of a young Japanese couple. Their daughter, they tell me, is complaining about the harshness of her first grade teacher.

3. Travel has taught me that despite all the exotic differences of dress and language, of political and religious beliefs, that all the world's people are essentially alike. We all have

the same urges and concerns; we all yearn for the same goals. And those who patronize other people, or demonize those with whom they disagree, or regard them as funny or backward, are foolish, indeed; they have not yet learned the lessons of travel.

4 **We all think ourselves virtuous:** At the bar of an Amsterdam cafe, I am talking with a Dutch friend. Last night, he tells me, a nationwide telethon had raised the equivalent of 40-some-odd million dollars for cancer research. "Only in Holland," he says, "could such results be obtained."

5 We all think ourselves the best, we all believe with great sincerity in the superiority of our own nation and culture, as compared with others. How many times have you heard politicians proclaim this nation or that nation to be the finest on earth? Travel rids you of that smug chauvinism; it exposes you to the finest in every land, and makes you distinctly uneasy — as it now does me — when you later return home and hear people proclaiming their own nation to be better than others.

6 **We are all responsible for one another:** It is the early 1980s. Dancing down a broad boulevard of Zagreb comes a succession of laughing, gaily-clad groups gathered there for a nationwide folk-dance festival of Yugoslavia. At the curb, I stand watching Muslims and Christians, Bosnians, Croatians and Serbs, celebrating in complete harmony. In later years, and because of travel, I remember them as distinct physical presences, not as abstractions; I get physically ill when I read of the violence between them. I feel the same intimate bond with the Protestants and Catholics of northern Ireland, whose cities I visited at the height of the "troubles," and with people of both Egypt and Israel, to which I once led groups of tourists. Travel makes it impossible to pay no heed to the sufferings of others, simply because they are far away; it erases distance, and makes you a more sensitive citizen of the world, yearning for peace everywhere.

7 **We grow when we confront our political or religious opposites:** I am at a residential yoga community, opening my mind to non-linear thinking. And though the guru's speech is directly at odds with my usual rationalism, I find myself enjoying it, and savoring this clash of new ideas. Another time I am at a "personal growth center" on the West Coast, in a class of "encounter therapy." I am told that I must clasp hands with the elderly gentleman opposite me, look deeply into his eyes, wish him well, give him a bear hug. And though I am initially loathe to do so, I then feel a surge of shame that I have allowed myself to be so emotionally controlled that I cannot offer sympathy to a fellow human being.

8 Travel exposes you to ideas, lifestyles, theologies and philosophies that challenge your most cherished beliefs. It takes you out of a setting in which everyone thinks the same, and sends you into the unknown, to your political or religious opposites, your "adversaries." Travel has made me confront my "opposites."

9 **More than a single answer exists for human problems:** I am walking the streets of Hong Kong, past signs for herbal medicines and acupuncturists. And all around are millions of people perfectly content with these approaches to personal health so different from our own. Another time I am lying in a copper bathtub filled with naturally-carbonated water, in a baths establishment of the Belgian city of Spa. And though my mind tells me it can't be, that this reliance on "water cures" is scientific rubbish, I feel

something happening to my body, and begin to suspect that the three hundred million Europeans who believe in such remedies may not be wrong.

10. Travel teaches you that a whole range of unusual practices may work in differing contexts; it suggest new approaches for your own society, keeps you open to novel proposals and experiments in every field.

11. **All people should be "minorities":** I walk the great cities of China, and gradually realize that in their midst, I am a minority in the same way that others are minorities in the city where I live. And I feel, as so many other travelers have felt, the gradual weakening of whatever racist impulses still inhabit my sub-conscious. Travel teaches the absurdity of reacting to people according to their color. It makes everyone a minority on occasion. And people who come back from such trips are often changed by the experience, as I have been.

12. Travel, for many, is a mere recreation. But travel is also education, perhaps the best form of education. Certainly, it impacts the mind in a way that sometimes no other activity — even that of widespread reading — can quite do. It has changed my life, and made me a different sort of person.

13. We are the first generation in human history to be able to travel to other continents as easily as we once took a trolley to the next town. Dare we hope that a more understanding, more tolerant and peaceful individual will be brought about by that development?

Source: Arthur Frommer's Budget Travel Website

VOCABULARY

Use Context Clues

1. Is *rid* (paragraph 5) a noun, verb, or adverb? _____

   Define *rid*. _____

2. What is the meaning of the word *curb* in paragraph 6? _____

3. Define *clasp* (paragraph 7). _____

4. Find a word in paragraph 7 that means "to be unwilling or unhappy."
   _____

5. What does the expression *in their midst* mean? (See paragraph 11)
   _____

COMPREHENSION

Find main and supporting ideas

1. How is the author an authority on this subject?
   _____

2 For each of the author's main points, he includes at least one example. Briefly summarize an example for each point. (Use your own words)

EXAMPLE:

We are all alike: *A Japanese couple worry about their daughter's teacher.*

a) We all think ourselves virtuous: _____

b) We are all responsible for one another: _____

c) We grow when we confront our opposites: _____

d) More than a single answer exists for human problems: _____

e) All people should be minorities: _____

3 Look at the introduction to this text. What is the author's thesis? In other words, what main point is he trying to make?

_____
_____
_____

WATCHING: Village of Idiots

You will watch an NFB film that is based on an old Jewish folktale. This seemingly simple story about an old fool contains complex messages about the human condition.

WATCHING COMPREHENSION

Take notes as you watch the film, and then answer the questions.

1 At the beginning of the video, how does Schmendrik seem to feel about his wife and children?

_____
_____

2 Why does Schmendrik want to leave his town of Chelm?

_____

_____

3 What does Schmendrik discover when he travels?

_____

_____

4 How does Schmendrik change?

_____

_____

5 *Schmendrik* is a Yiddish word that means "a humorous overachiever who gets more than he deserves." It also means "someone who holds unrealistic hope." How is Schmendrik's name appropriate for this story?

_____

_____

_____

6 This tale, on the surface, is about a foolish and confused old man who gets "lost." But this seemingly simple folktale also provides us with lessons about the human condition. What three lessons does the story illustrate?

_____

_____

_____

Discuss your answers with your classmates.

WRITTEN RESPONSE

Compare *The Village of Idiots* and "How Travel Changed My Life." Answer each question in paragraph form. Your paragraphs should have about eight to ten sentences each.

1 Briefly summarize the story of *The Village of Idiots*. What happens in this film?

2 Both *The Village of Idiots* and "How Travel Changed My Life" contain messages or morals for the reader/viewer. What messages are the same? What messages are contradictory?

3 Think about some of the lessons that Arthur Frommer ("How Travel Changed My Life") and Schmendrik learned. Write a paragraph about an incident in your life in which you learned a lesson that is similar to one of them.

Travel Stories from Syria

Heather Burles got the travel bug and went to the ancient city of Damascus, in Syria. Despite the culture shock and, at times, dangerous situations, Heather returned with a new appreciation for that foreign land. She has written a book about her experiences called *Smoldering Incense, Hammered Brass*.

In an interview for CBC radio, Heather discusses her journey.

LISTENING COMPREHENSION

Answer the following questions.

1. In Canada, what kind of work did Heather do? _____

2. Why did Heather go to Syria?
   _____
   _____

3. Why did Heather decide to get a one-way ticket? _____
   _____

4. What happened when she arrived at her hotel?
   _____
   _____

5. Heather said that she had very few problems as a single woman traveling in Syria. What two things did she do to minimize the chances of having problems?

   a) _____

   b) _____

6. She did have problems with some men. Who were they, and why did they treat her differently?
   _____
   _____

7. According to Heather, why do some Syrian men think that Western women are amoral?
   _____
   _____

8. When Heather's boyfriend came to Syria, how did Heather present him to people?
   _____

How did men treat Heather differently when her boyfriend was in Syria?

9. Heather was at a Bedouin feast and she was offered sheep's tongue. How did she handle the situation?

Descriptive Language

Most essay writing contains a certain amount of descriptive prose. With language, the writer is able to arouse our senses so that we can see, hear, smell, taste, or feel what the writer is expressing. As you read the following essay, notice the descriptive language.

READING 1.2

The Passenger

by Julie Nehme

A train in India.

1. I am a big-city girl and I like things to click along efficiently. My job in Toronto is stressful and fast-paced, so last March, when my three-week vacation came up, I decided to try something totally new and exotic. Impulsively I booked a flight to India. Little did I know that my high-speed lifestyle was on a collision course with an ancient civilization.

2. After a week in the New Delhi area, I booked a train ticket to Madras.

3. When I got inside the train, I walked down the aisle until I saw a compartment with three women in it. The three women sat silently, staring at my maneuvers, their hands clasped on their laps.

4. The train left the station at 8 AM and rattled along for about two hours. While the women chatted, I tried to appreciate the landscape but my thoughts kept returning to my workload. After about one hour, I finally managed to get some rest.

5. Suddenly my back slammed against the seat as the train jerked to a stop. I jumped up, certain that we had arrived. A solemn conductor passed by, announcing that there would be a delay.

6. I sat for about twenty minutes and felt increasingly irritated. I stopped a man in the corridor and asked, "Why aren't we moving?" He shrugged and walked away.

7. I went onto the train platform and asked others, frantically, "When will we go again?" Nobody seemed to know exactly what had happened. No one seemed to care.

8. I was antsy. I only had two weeks left of my vacation and didn't want to waste time waiting.

9. Vendors floated by on the small platform beside the train. "Chai — chai — chai," the tea sellers hollered.

10. "Muri-pan, muri-pan," a woman repeated, over and over, as she tried to sell her puffed rice snacks.

11. Most of the passengers had disembarked and many were crouching outside the train smoking beedies (little wrapped tobacco leaves) and staring peacefully off into the distance. They remained remarkably complacent even after an hour had passed.

12. In America there would have been yelling and fistfights by now. But here, everybody just…waited. I wanted to shake people. I wanted to get to Madras. I wanted to be anywhere but on a train that wasn't moving.

13. News filtered among the passengers; the delay may be for several more hours. I paid a few rupees for a cup of steaming milky tea and admired the hand-crafted reddish clay cup. When I finished, I watched the tea-seller's child crush some used cups into the soil.

14. The sun was high above us when a small child came to sit beside me. She asked, over and over, "What is your name?" tasting the English words on her tongue. I repeated my name, "Julie," each time, until we were both mesmerized by the exercise. Julie — Julie — Julie-Julie-JulieJuliejuliejulie …

15. The three Indian women who had been in my train compartment were sitting on a bench. One of them waved her hand, asking me to join them. The ladies had baskets of food and large red clay jugs filled with water. They spoke very little English, so we spoke with eyes and smiles and I was offered food. As I ate a piece of mango, the sweet gooey juice stuck to my cheeks and chin. There were just tastes and sweet smells and flashing teeth under shy smiles.

16. It was a fine moment. I started to enjoy myself.

17. I thanked the women for the food and arose, indicating that I would now go for a walk.

18. I walked to the front end of the train and sat on the ground. A woman near me had spread out a blanket and lay on it with her baby. Even the baby was peaceful. I sat, watching them. When the woman stood up, the sari that she had slept in remained remarkably unwrinkled, the material unfolding and falling in silken drapes. She expertly bundled up her baby and, with her free hand, she rolled the blanket into a tight ball.

19. I drank more tea. I watched the sun lower in the sky, turning the walls of a neighboring village pink. I was completely content.

20 Like this, *an entire day passed.*

21 The sky was dark when the conductor announced that we would continue on our way. The crowds of people murmured, leisurely picking up bundles and then trudging back into the train. I returned to my seat. In a few minutes, the bare light bulb above me began to sway and I listened to the pounding, singing wheels.

22 It was a remarkable day. I had learned a valuable lesson; I had learned the art of waiting.

VOCABULARY

Use Context Clues

Define each of the following terms. Do not use your dictionary. Use context clues in the text.

TERM OR EXPRESSION	PARAGRAPH NUMBER	DEFINITION
1. to book	1	
2. aisle	3	
3. to clasp	3	
4. to slam	5	
5. antsy	8	
6. to holler	9	
7. rupee	13	
8. to bundle	18	
9. to sway	21	

COMPREHENSION

Recognizing Description

The text uses many descriptive sentences. For each of the following senses, find a quotation in which that sense is aroused. Highlight that quotation.

| touch | sight | sound | smell |

Find the Main Idea

1 Who is the text about? _____

② When does the action occur? (If you can't find a specific time reference in the text, ask yourself when it occurs in the author's life.)
_____

③ Where does the action take place? _____

④ What happens? _____
_____
_____

⑤ How does the main character change? _____

⑥ The main idea is the most important or central idea of a text. To find out the main idea of this narrative essay, combine your answers from numbers **1** to **5**. Write a statement of main idea.
_____
_____
_____

Writing Tip: Using Descriptive Language

We often get into a rut when we write. We use the same nouns, verbs, and adjectives over and over. Try the following exercise alone or with a partner. Work on expanding your vocabulary. You may need a good dictionary or thesaurus for this activity.

Part 1: Look at the descriptions. Write the letter of the alternative verbs that mean the same thing as the verb + adverb combination.

ORDINARY VOCABULARY		VIVID, DESCRIPTIVE VERBS
1. to laugh quietly	_F_	A. whisper, mutter
2. to walk slowly	____	B. shout, yell, holler
3. to cry loudly	____	C. whimper, sniffle, weep
4. to speak loudly	____	D. shuffle, saunter, stroll
5. to speak softly	____	E. bawl, scream, wail
6. to cry quietly	____	F. giggle, chuckle

Part 2: Examine the following sentences. Each sentence contains an italicized verb or adjective. Find at least two synonyms for the italicized term.

EXAMPLE: That is **good** food: _tasty, delicious_

1. Ali is a *pretty* woman. _____
2. Jeremy hurts others. He is a *bad* person. _____
3. I *thought* about the problem all day. _____
4. We watched a really *good* movie. _____
5. I felt *surprised* when I won the lottery. _____
6. He is a *nice* person. _____
7. I *ran* to work. _____
8. When the strange man made a vulgar comment, she *hit* him. _____

WRITING SUGGESTION

Think about an important moment in your life. Write a short narrative essay about that moment. Try to use descriptive language to create a mood or to express vividly the emotions you were experiencing. Make sure that you have a clearly identifiable topic sentence. With a highlighter pen, highlight descriptive words and phrases.

SPEAKING

Life Experience

Prepare a presentation about an experience that changed your life. If you have trouble coming up with ideas, ask yourself the following questions:

— Have I ever done something really positive (forgiven someone, helped someone, stopped taking someone for granted, etc.) or really negative (cheated, lied, excluded someone, ridiculed someone, etc.)?

— Has anyone near me ever had an experience that taught me a lesson?

— Has any story, movie, or real-life news event had a profound impact on me and changed me in some way?

After you have an idea for your story, choose one of the proverbs listed in this chapter or find your own proverb or quotation. (Some "quotation" Internet addresses appear at the end of this chapter.) Link that proverb to your story. You could include that proverb in your introduction or conclusion.

Remember:

■ Your presentation should be 3 to 5 minutes in length.

■ You may use cue cards that contain key words and phrases. Do not read your text!

Practice your presentation but don't memorize it. (If you recite a memorized text, it can sound very unnatural.)

These sites have great "quotations" or "proverbs" pages.
www.famous-quotations.com/
www.quotegarden.com
www.creativequotations.com

If any of these addresses are no longer in service, just go to a search engine and type in *"quotations and proverbs."*

The following sites have travel stories, tips, and information.
Arthur Frommer's budget travel website
www.frommers.com

Journey Women is an online travel magazine for women.
www.journeywoman.com

CHAPTER 2 Skeptical Minds

You can't reason someone out of a position he didn't reason himself into.
—Anonymous

The believer is happy; the doubter is wise.
—Hungarian Proverb

Think about these quotations. What do they mean?

Every day we are bombarded with information by the media, parents, teachers, and friends. How can we determine what to believe? And does it matter if we believe in things that may not be true? This chapter examines *fact vs. fantasy*.

Fact or Fantasy?

Survey some classmates. Get into a team of about five students to answer the following questions.

1 Are the following statements true or false? In the space provided, indicate how many of you think the statement is a fact and how many think it is fantasy.

	FACT	FANTASY
a. It is possible to create a society where everybody has equal wealth.		
b. Reincarnation is true: we have all had past lives.		
c. Every person has the potential to be evil.		
d. Some psychics and mediums can contact the dead.		
e. The universe is expanding.		
f. People have mysteriously disappeared in the Bermuda Triangle.		
g. Capital punishment helps to lower the crime rate.		
h. Horoscopes provide useful information about future events.		

	FACT	FANTASY
i. Global warming is serious and threatens life on earth.		
j. Princess Diana's death was no "accident"; she was murdered.		
k. Psychics can help police solve crimes.		
l. Human beings have walked on the moon.		
m. If all children were deeply loved, none would become criminals.		
n. People are safer when they have guns in their homes.		
o. Some people can see the future.		
p. Aliens have visited the earth and kidnapped some people.		

2 Are any items on the list definitely factual? Which one(s)? _____

3 Are any items definitely fantasies? Which one(s)? _____
Explain what influences your beliefs.

JFK: What's Fact, What's Not

(Warning to teachers: the video contains actual footage from the Zapruder film of Kennedy's assassination. The graphic nature of this footage could be upsetting.)

One of the biggest mysteries of the twentieth century surrounds the death of an American president. Who killed John Fitzgerald Kennedy? No generally accepted "truth" has emerged, and some say we will never know what happened on November 22, 1963, at 12:30 PM.

The strongest evidence is the now famous eight-millimetre home movie footage of the actual assassination taken by a man named Abraham Zapruder. This piece of evidence along with eyewitness accounts have led many people to propose various conspiracy theories. Some suggest that the FBI, the CIA, pro-Castro Cubans, anti-Castro Cubans, the Mafia, and even other politicians were involved.

PRE-WATCHING DISCUSSION

Before you watch:

1 With your classmates, discuss what you already know about the assassination.

2 Review the following information.

John F. Kennedy → He was the youngest president of the United States. He was visiting Dallas prior to his 1964 re-election campaign.

Lee Harvey Oswald → He was a U.S. citizen and former Marine. After a brief period living in Russia, Oswald got a job at the Book Depository in Dallas.

Lyndon Johnson → He was the vice-president and the man who took over the government after Kennedy was assassinated.

Jack Ruby → He was a nightclub owner who was dying of cancer. He shot Oswald.

Jim Garrison → He was the District Attorney for the city of New Orleans. He believed the Kennedy assassination was a conspiracy.

Warren Commission → A commission, named after Justice Earl Warren, was set up after the assassination to determine what had happened.

WATCHING

Watch the film. Take notes about the facts of the case and then answer the following questions.

1 Describe the conclusions of the Warren Commission.

   a) Who shot Kennedy? _____

   b) How many bullets were shot? _____

   c) What direction did the bullets come from? _____

   d) Where did the bullets land? _____

   _____

   _____

   _____

2 List some facts and theories about the assassination.

   a) How soon after the assassination was Oswald arrested? _____

   b) Where was Oswald killed? _____

   c) How many seconds did the shooting of Kennedy last? _____

   d) What direction did the bullets probably come from? _____

   e) How many shots were probably fired? _____

3 Why was one bullet was called "magic"? _____

_____

_____

Skeptical Minds

4 What suspicious events involved Kennedy's body? _____
_____
_____

5 What are some problems with the Warren Commission report?
_____
_____
_____
_____
_____
_____
_____

6 According to the evidence presented in the video, was Oswald the lone assassin of President Kennedy? If you disagree with the Warren Commission, give at least three reasons why.
_____
_____
_____
_____
_____
_____

(To the teacher: Alternate questions appear in the Instructor's Manual.)

POST-WATCHING DISCUSSION

1 Will the truth ever come out about the Kennedy assassination? Why or why not?

2 In a *New York Times* article, Stephen E. Ambrose claimed that conspiracy theories are linked to political agendas. What other conspiracy theories do you know about? Could conspiracy theories be dangerous? Explain why.

Moments in Time

There are historical moments that become frozen in time. People who lived through a startling moment generally recollect where they were when the event happened.

Look at the following list of historical moments. Most occurred before you were born. With a partner or a team of students, try to identify as many of the following historical moments as possible.

_____ • **April 18, 1906.** This natural disaster shook a west-coast city.

_____ • **April 15, 1912.** It was considered unsinkable. Then it sank.

_____ • **June 28, 1914.** The assassination of Archduke Franz Ferdinand caused this event.

_____ • **November 7, 1917.** For Vladimir, it was the beginning, not the end.

_____ • **November 11, 1918.** In Canada, we remember this moment each year at the same hour, on the same day, in the same month.

_____ • **1928.** Fleming changed the course of modern medicine with this invention.

_____ • **October 24, 1929.** This crash was heard around the world.

_____ • **December 11, 1936.** He gave up a royal job for the woman he loved.

_____ • **November 8, 1938.** The sound of breaking glass foretold the horrors to come.

_____ • **December 7, 1941.** This moment, said Roosevelt, "will live in infamy."

_____ • **August 6, 1945.** "Little Boy" was dropped on a Japanese city.

_____ • **1947.** Tommy Douglas, Saskatchewan Premier, launched this system.

_____ • **January 30, 1948.** This spiritual leader was a stirring symbol of non-violence, and he died violently.

_____ • **May 14, 1948.** A homeland at last.

_____ • **May 29, 1953.** Tensing Norgay and a New Zealander reached the top of the world.

_____ • **August 5, 1962.** A beautiful blond, originally named Norma Jeane, died.

_____ • **April 4, 1968.** The greatest voice for civil rights was killed.

_____ • **July 20, 1969.** His giant leap was actually one small step.

_____ • **May 1977.** A new music movement began with the song "God Save the Queen." The song cover featured a picture of the British queen with a safety pin through her nose.

_____ • **August 16, 1977.** The king died in the bathroom of his mansion.

_____ • **July 25, 1978.** Baby Louise was born and made medical history.

_____ • **December 8, 1980.** A deluded gunman killed a legendary musician in New York.

Skeptical Minds

- _____ • **January 28, 1986.** A televised fiery ball reminded us that space travel is dangerous.
- _____ • **June 4, 1989.** Tanks rolled over protesters.
- _____ • **November 9, 1989.** This structure that had divided a city came tumbling down.
- _____ • **April 8, 1994.** A frail, talented, former "teen spirit" died in his Seattle mansion.
- _____ • **January 1997.** A sheep hit the papers and began an ethical debate.
- _____ • **July 1, 1997.** Britain gave up its claim to this small but prosperous Asian port.
- _____ • **August 31, 1997.** Mountains of flowers commemorated her death.
- _____ • **September 5, 1997.** Her birth name was Agnes Bojaxhiu. This Yugoslavian nun took her last breath.
- _____ • **September 11, 2001.** Complacency was shattered.

Note: Many of these historical facts appeared in CBC TV's *News In Review Resource Guide*, March 1992.

DISCUSSION

1. What three events in the list are the most historically important and will be remembered hundreds of years from now?

2. What events in the list have generated a lot of fantasy since they happened?

3. What other events that took place in the past five years could become frozen moments in time?

Reading Tip: Determine Bias

Everyone has bias. Our age, gender, racial, financial, and cultural background may influence our opinions about issues. Nonetheless, newspaper and magazine writers often try to appear objective when they write informative articles.

Look at the differences between subjective and objective writing.

IN SUBJECTIVE WRITING, THE AUTHOR:	IN OBJECTIVE WRITING, THE AUTHOR:
• expresses a point of view • may express personal feelings (*I think…*) • may make statements that are one-sided (*animal testing is evil*) • may give advice (*You should never drink and drive*) • may ask rhetorical questions (*How can we stop this slaughter?*) • may use emotionally loaded language (*She abandoned her son*)	• masks his/her feelings and appears neutral • describes facts without commenting on those facts • quotes the opinions of others, not his/her own

Chapter 2

Be careful. Sometimes writing that appears objective could be biased. For example, if an author disagrees with capital punishment, he could choose to interview people who also disagree with it and he could leave out contradictory information. Thus, even though he doesn't state his opinion, there is a bias.

As you read, you can ask yourself if the author is expressing his or her point of view. Try to recognize bias.

Reading Exercise

Look at the following excerpts, and then answer the questions that follow.

Sample 1

The *Medical Post* reported in its Apr. 28 edition that a large number of people are dying due to adverse drug reactions even when drugs are used as intended. Why are alternative medical practitioners, such as chiropractors, denigrated for a small number of accidents, when the death rate for those who see a regular general practitioner is so much higher? The population has a right to know that alternative medicine is no more dangerous than conventional medicine.

1. Is this text an example of objective or subjective writing? _____
Highlight a sentence from the text as proof of your choice.

2. What main point is the author probably trying to make?
_____

3. Is the author biased, and if so, how? _____

Sample 2

According to Richard Kerwin, a lawyer with Fineman and Grey, the legal profession is not as glamorous as it may seem. "We watch programs like *Perry Mason* or *Law and Order* and we expect that a lawyer's life is exciting. We see the thrilling courtroom scenes. What we don't see is the drudgery involved in a lawyer's work life." Richard says that he spends most of his days researching the many cases that he is working on. "I spend most of my time looking through law books. I spend very little time in the courtroom," he says.

Divorce lawyer Berry Brendon agrees with Richard. "The people we meet in this profession are in a traumatic period of their lives. It is emotionally draining to deal with them." Both lawyers suggest that students who want to enter the legal profession have a realistic view of the job.

1. Is this text an example of objective or subjective writing? _____
Highlight a sentence from the text as proof of your choice.

2. What main point is the author probably trying to make?
_____

3. Is the author biased, and if so, how? _____

Skeptical Minds

PAIR READING ACTIVITY (optional)

Find a partner. One of you could read "Ghost in My House," and the other could read "The Mesmerizer." Both texts are written in the narrative style (each text tells a story) and both contain messages for the reader.

You will answer the questions that follow your reading with a team of students. Later, you will share information with your partner.

READING 2.1

Bertram Rothschild is a recently retired clinical psychologist. He has published twenty short stories and some of his recent essays have appeared in the *Humanist* and *Freethought Today*. In the following text, Rothschild confronts a ghost, or does he?

The Ghost in My House

by Bertram Rothschild

1. For a while, I (almost) believed a ghost occupied my house. Before I confess all, however, you need to know something about me. First, I'm approaching (not there yet) my **dotage**; second, I'm a clinical psychologist; and third, I was a skeptic well before I knew the word, much less its meaning. If asked about ESP and the spirit world, I would laugh and wonder about what kind of idiot could believe such things. The arguments I've had with believers sometimes almost led to blows, though in my later decades I decided that keeping my mouth shut was wise. But, with further maturity, I concluded that the wisest course of action would be to focus my skepticism on issues of public concern.

2. Here's the story: I lay in bed one evening, half dozing, with the bedroom door shut. My wife gets to bed later than I do, but sometimes she'll come in to find something and then leave, again shutting the door. You must understand: this is a decades-old pattern, one with which I am quite familiar. Well, as I lay there, I heard her footsteps approaching the door. I saw the door open with exactly the same speed as always, and it opened to the same distance as usual. I expected to hear her footsteps coming into the room, but there was no such sound. (As I write this, I realize that I did not hear her footsteps. It was an after-the-fact embellishment obviously supportive of the ghost theory.)

3. My first assumption was that she had changed her mind, but two considerations suggest otherwise. First, she would have closed the door, and second, there were no footsteps leading away. Okay, it wasn't her so it must have been a puff of wind. But the night was calm and no window was open. The puff of wind hypothesis dissolved.

4. Now in some consternation, I arose and looked for her. She was not in a nearby room, not anywhere on the bedroom level. I walked further to the little balcony that overlooks the downstairs area and there I saw her, with a bowl of cereal and thoroughly ensconced in a crossword puzzle. Although the circumstances convinced me it could not have been her, I asked. She denied having anything to do with the door that had mysteriously opened and went back to the puzzle. Although she has at times been a trickster, she would always give me a clue about her intent to tease me. Without a triumphant grin on her face, she clearly had not tried to disconcert me.

dotage
old age

5. When I described the door's peculiar behavior she jokingly asked if I thought it were a ghost. I snickered at her and returned to bed. A ghost? Ridiculous. I soon fell asleep. The next morning, dozing in bed, I became aware of the noises – and she did too. One of us said: "Perhaps it was the ghost." We both laughed, but we both listened for more strange sounds. And, of course, they were there.

6. That evening, in the den watching television, we both heard sort of a combined clink and thud clearly indicating that some hard object had fallen to the floor. I examined the area and could find nothing to account for the sound. Were we disquieted? You bet. The noises continued over several days. We jokingly got into the habit of evoking the ghost as explanation … and I started to take that explanation seriously. As a consequence, the hairs on my arms would stand up when I could not find an explanation for some sound or event.

7. At the same time, I resisted the "ghost" explanation and wondered about my willingness to accept the possibility. The noises, after all, were really nothing new, just the creaks and groans of the house. They had always been there, but rarely the focus of my attention. Either every house I'd ever visited had a resident ghost (possible, but surely unlikely), or house noises were commonplace, not the production of invisible spirits. But the door incident remained on my mind. I realized, finally, that my mind, operating out of awareness, *demanded* an explanation of the door's behavior. It wasn't the wind; it wasn't my wife. What the hell was it? I *had* to know; but only the ghost hypothesis remained.

8. I had made the same error that humans have made since our cave-dwelling ancestors roamed the earth. When rational explanation failed to settle the matter, they invoked spirits and magical events. Any explanation would be better than chaos and, if one could invoke the spirits, it implied power over ugly reality. And we are the genetic inheritors of what worked for survival.

9. No, I don't believe that a ghost opened the door, but that I had entertained the possibility continues to astonish me. Without an understanding of the event, my brain simply created a magical explanation despite my years of looking at the universe in a rational way. We all do that. Our brains fill in the blanks, and without considerable debunking effort we fall prey to such "explanations." Children do this all the time; and for many people nothing changes with age – they continue to explain events with their idiosyncratic construction of explanations that have nothing to do with reality.

10. Albert Ellis, a highly esteemed psychologist, has suggested that human beings 1) have a strong tendency to be irrational, and 2) have a strong tendency to ignore data contrary to their beliefs. However, this can be overcome by training in critical thinking. That is the essence of his psychotherapy: teaching people how to think about their beliefs regarding reality. We need to teach our children how to think and reason at the earliest age possible, a process that should be ongoing.

11. When I was a child, I asked my mother to tell me how lightning and thunder are produced. She explained that clouds bumped into each other, producing a spark and noise. I won't tell you how old I was before I figured it out. But, how many more subtle explanations have I (or you) lived by, never noticing their absurdity?

Answer the following questions with a team of students who have also read this story.

VOCABULARY

Define the following terms. Try to use context clues instead of relying on your dictionary.

VOCABULARY TERM	PARAGRAPH NUMBER	DEFINITION
1. blows	1	
2. to doze	2	
3. puff	3	
4. to be ensconced	4	
5. to snicker	5	
6. to be disquieted	6	
7. commonplace	7	
8. to roam	8	
9. prey	9	
10. to overcome	10	

COMPREHENSION

Discover Bias

1 Describe the author. Use at least five adjectives in your description.

_____
_____

2 What happened after the author heard the door open? In point form, describe the events and the stages in the author's thinking process.

He heard the door open.

_____
_____
_____
_____
_____
_____
_____

3 At the end of the story, how has the author's opinion about ghosts changed?
_____

4 What was the author's profession? _____
How could his profession have influenced his opinion about ghosts? _____
_____

5 Does the author have a bias? If so, what is his bias? _____
_____

6 According to the author, why do people believe in mysterious things such as ghosts?
_____
_____
_____

7 What is the main message, or lesson, that we can learn from this text? _____
_____
_____

READING 2.2

Mark Twain is most famous for his books *The Adventures of Tom Sawyer* (1876) and *The Adventures of Huckleberry Finn* (1885). This adapted selection originally appeared in Twain's autobiography.

The Mesmerizer

by Mark Twain (1835-1910)

1. An exciting event in our village was the arrival of the mesmerizer. He advertised his show, and promised marvels. Not many people attended, the first night, but next day they had so many wonders to tell that everybody's curiosity was fired, and after that for a **fortnight** the magician had prosperous times.

   fortnight two weeks

2. I was fourteen or fifteen years old — the age at which a boy is willing to endure all things if he can be conspicuous and show off before the public. When I saw the "subjects" perform their foolish antics on the platform and make the people laugh and shout and admire, I had a burning desire to be a subject myself. Every night, for three nights, I sat in the row of candidates on the platform, and held the magic disk in the palm of my hand, and gazed at it and tried to get sleepy, but it was a failure. I remained wide awake, and had to leave defeated, like the majority.

3. I had to sit there and envy Hicks; I had to sit there and see him jump when Simmons the enchanter exclaimed, "See the snake! see the snake!" and hear him say, "My, how beautiful!" in response to the suggestion that he was observing a splendid sunset; and so

on—the whole insane business. I couldn't laugh, I couldn't applaud; it filled me with bitterness to have people make a hero of Hicks, and crowd around him when the show was over. Hicks—the idea! I couldn't stand it.

4 On the fourth night temptation came, and I was not strong enough to resist. When I had gazed at the disk awhile I pretended to be sleepy. The professor came and he began to "draw" me with the disk, holding it in his fingers and telling me I could not take my eyes off it; so I rose slowly, bent and gazing, and followed that disk all over the place, just as I had seen the others do. Then I was put through the other paces. Upon suggestion I fled from snakes, passed buckets at a fire, kissed imaginary girls—and so on.

5 I was cautious at first, afraid the professor would discover that I was an impostor and drive me from the platform in disgrace; but as soon as I realized that I was not in danger, I set myself the task of terminating Hicks's usefulness as a subject, and of usurping his place.

6 It was a sufficiently easy task. Hicks saw what he saw; I saw more than was visible, and emptied the dictionary into it. Hicks had no imagination; I had a double supply.

7 At the end of my first half-hour Hicks was a thing of the past, a fallen hero, and I knew it and was glad. Whatever Hicks had failed in, I made it a point to succeed in. He had shown several bad defects, and I had made a note of them. For instance, if the magician asked, "What do you see?" and left him to invent a vision for himself, Hicks couldn't see a thing nor say a word, whereas the magician soon found that when it came to seeing stunning visions I could get along better without his help than with it.

8 Then there was another thing: whenever Simmons stood behind him and gazed at the back of his skull and tried to drive a mental suggestion into it, Hicks sat with vacant face, and never suspected. If he had been noticing, he could have seen by the **rapt** faces of the audience that something was going on behind his back that required a response.

rapt
attentive

9 I dreaded to have this test, for I knew the professor would be "willing" me to do something, and as I couldn't know what it was, I would be exposed and denounced. However, when my time came, I took my chance. I perceived by the tense and expectant faces of the people that Simmons was behind me willing me with all his might. I tried my best to imagine what he wanted, but nothing suggested itself. I felt ashamed and miserable, then. I believed that in another moment I should go out of that place disgraced. My next thought was how I could go out most sensationally and spectacularly.

10 There was a rusty and empty old revolver lying on the table, among the "properties" employed in the performances. On May Day, two or three weeks before, there had been a celebration by the schools, and I had had a quarrel with a big boy who was the school-bully. That boy was now seated in the middle of the house, halfway down the main aisle. I crept stealthily and impressively toward the table, with a dark and murderous scowl on my face, seized the revolver suddenly, shouted the bully's name, jumped off the platform, and made a rush for him and chased him out of the house before the paralyzed people could interfere to save him.

11 There was a storm of applause, and the magician, addressing the house, said, most impressively, "I assure you that without a single spoken word to guide him he has carried out what I mentally commanded him to do. I could have stopped him at a moment by

a mere exertion of my will, therefore the poor fellow who has escaped was at no time in danger."

12 So I was not in disgrace. I returned to the platform a hero. As regards mental suggestion, my fears of it were gone. Whenever I perceived that I was being willed to do something I got up and did something—anything that occurred to me—and the magician, not being a fool, always ratified it. When people asked me, "How can you tell what he is willing you to do?" I said, "It's just as easy," and they always said, admiringly, "Well it beats me how you can do it."

13 After that fourth night, that proud night, I was the only subject. Simmons invited no more candidates to the platform. I performed alone, every night, the rest of the fortnight. In the beginning of the second week I conquered the last doubters. Up to that time a dozen wise old heads, the intellectual aristocracy of the town, had held out as implacable unbelievers. I was as hurt by this as if I were engaged in some honest occupation. There is nothing surprising about this. Human beings feel dishonor the most, sometimes, when they most deserve it.

14 Those wise old gentlemen kept on shaking their heads all the first week, and saying they had seen no marvels there that could not have been produced by collusion. They were pretty **vain**, too, and liked to be superior to the ignorant and the gullible. Particularly old Dr. Peake. His opinion upon any matter was worth much more than that of any other person in the community. When I conquered him, at last, I knew I was undisputed master of the field; and now, after more than fifty years, I acknowledge, with a few dry old tears, that I **rejoiced** without shame.

vain
egotistical

rejoiced
celebrated

Answer the following questions with a team of students who have also read this story.

VOCABULARY

Define the following terms. Try to use context clues instead of relying on your dictionary.

VOCABULARY TERM	PARAGRAPH NUMBER	DEFINITION
1. antics	2	
2. to gaze	4	
3. imposter	5	
4. to ursurp	5	
5. skull	8	
6. to dread	9	
7. scowl	10	
8. mere	11	

Skeptical Minds

VOCABULARY TERM	PARAGRAPH NUMBER	DEFINITION
9. to ratify	12	
10. to hold out	13	

COMPREHENSION

1 What is a "mesmerizer"? _____

2 Use at least five adjectives to describe the author's character when he was a teenager.
_____

3 What happened after the author (Mark Twain) saw the magician? In point form, describe the events and the stages in Twain's thinking process.
He was jealous that Hicks got so much attention.
_____

4 What is the main difference between Twain and Hicks? _____

5 What type of person is Simmons (the mesmerizer)? Does he have special powers? Is he ethical?
_____

6 Why did Twain "rejoice without shame" (paragraph 14)? _____

7 What does Twain suggest about "magic" and mesmerizers? _____

Chapter 2

8 What message or lesson can you learn from Twain's story? _____

PAIR READING: SHARE YOUR INFORMATION

Compare "Ghost in My House" and "The Mesmerizer." Do the following:

- Share vocabulary definitions. Fill in the definitions of terms that follow the story you didn't read.
- Tell your partner about your story. What happened?
- What lesson can you learn from each story?

READING 2.3

Orson Welles was an artist, actor, playwright, director, producer, and radio star. When he was just 21 he formed the Mercury Theater and he performed radio plays and Broadway shows. He is most renowned for two things: he wrote, acted in, directed and produced the film *Citizen Kane* and, at the tender age of 22, he presented the radio drama, *War of the Worlds*.

As you read the following text, keep in mind that radio was a relatively new and powerful medium, and also remember that television was not yet a fixture in people's homes.

The Night the Martians Attacked

Lee Krystek

1. It was a quiet Sunday night in greater New York City: October 30th, 1938: "mischief night." Thirty-two million people sat down by their radios to tune in and catch their favorite shows.

2. *Charlie McCarthy* was on at 8 o'clock. About ten minutes into the program a singer who was "less than compelling" took the microphone. This resulted in a number of people changing the dial, mid-show. At WABC, in New York, they found what was apparently a program of dance music: Ramon Raquello and his orchestra from the Meridian Room of the Park Plaza Hotel.

3. Suddenly the broadcast was interrupted by a series of news bulletins: A large meteor had impacted in New Jersey near Grover's Mill. The object turned out not to be a meteor, but a metal cylinder. The cylinder opened and Martians, driving huge fighting machines, emerged. They were advancing upon New York City.

4. Within thirty minutes the voice of a radio reporter, supposedly covering the event from a window in Manhattan, told of a gas attack on the city:

5. *Smoke comes out…black smoke, drifting over the city. People in the streets see it now. They're running towards the East River… thousands of them, dropping like rats. Now the smoke's spreading faster. It's reached Times Square. People are trying to run away from it, but it's no*

Skeptical Minds

use. They're falling like flies. Now the smoke's crossing Sixth Avenue... Fifth Avenue... one hundred yards away... it's fifty feet...

6. Then the reporter stopped talking. There was silence for a few seconds. Then the plaintive cry of a ham radio operator:

7. *Isn't there anyone on the air? Isn't there anyone?*

8. Many people panicked. They ran out in the streets ready to evacuate the city. Others called relatives on the telephone to warn them. Some called the police. A few simply broke down in tears. Apparently not many of them listened to what came next on the radio: An announcement that they had been listening to a *Mercury Theatre on the Air* production of H.G. Well's *War of the Worlds.*

9. Many years after the event Orson Welles, the producer of the Mercury Theatre, claimed he had "merrily anticipated" the kind of response the program drew.

10. The *Mercury Theatre on the Air*, like most radio shows in those days, was done live. It was also broadcast across the United States on the Columbia Broadcasting System. The program started with an opening narration by Orson Welles himself, then switched to the dance music which was then interrupted by the bulletins. By the time the script had reached the point of black smoke obliterating the city, the cast knew something was up. The CBS switchboard was jammed with calls.

11. The next day the newspapers reported that thousands of people called the police, newspapers and radio stations throughout cities in the United States and Canada. Evening worship services in some churches were interrupted by the news and a few turned into "end of the world" prayer meetings. At St. Michael's Hospital in Newark fifteen people were treated for shock and hysteria, a scene repeated throughout New York area medical facilities. Some people claimed that the radio show had nearly given them a heart attack.

12. Because the broadcast had been carried throughout the country, the effect was nationwide. Listeners in the Western United States, though not fearing immediate danger for themselves, called relatives and friends back east who had not heard the program. This further fueled the panic.

13. The following day the public was indignant. CBS said it might drop the *Mercury Theatre on the Air* from its lineup. Perhaps even more frightening than a real alien invasion was a proposal by Senator Herring of Iowa that all future radio broadcasts be reviewed by the government before presentation.

14. Many lawsuits were prepared but the radio network was able to defend itself by pointing to the multiple announcements made during the program reminding listeners that what they were hearing was a radio drama.

15. In the end the major effect of the broadcast was to increase the ratings of the *Mercury Theatre on the Air* and catapult Orson Well's career farther forward.

16. Why did it affect people so deeply? It may have been because the "live" bulletin seemed to interrupt the news, confusing people about what was real and what was not.

17 The public was undoubtedly also jittery because of the political situation in Europe. In only three more years the United States would be drawn into World War II. Just a month before, a crisis in Munich had been covered on the radio with the same type of bulletins used in the broadcast.

18 Could it happen again? Many suggest that the public is now much too media savvy to be fooled by such a hoax. But consider this: In September of 1996 hundreds of people in Madrid, Spain were panicked by television "news" broadcasts depicting giant saucers hovering over United States landmarks. The segments turned out to be clever advertisements for a new alien invasion movie, *Independence Day*.

VOCABULARY AND COMPREHENSION

Define the following terms. Use context clues to help you.

1. plaintive (paragraph 6) _____

2. jittery (paragraph 17) _____

3. hovering (paragraph 18) _____

4. Find a word in paragraph 10 that means "congested or blocked." _____

5. This text is:

    a) subjective   b) objective

6. What techniques did Welles use to make the Martian Attack seem realistic?

   _____
   _____
   _____

7. Was Welles purposely trying to cause citizens to panic? Explain your answer and find a supporting quotation from the text.

   _____
   _____
   _____

8. Why was the public so easily fooled, and why were people so "indignant" after the radio play aired?

   _____
   _____
   _____
   _____

9 Why does the author call Senator Herring's proposal "more frightening than a real alien invasion"? (See paragraph 13.)

_____

_____

10 In your opinion, are people today less easily manipulated by the media, or are they as gullible as people were in 1938? Think of a specific example to support your point.

_____

_____

_____

_____

11 What does "The Night the Martians Attacked" story tell us about human nature?

_____

_____

_____

DISCUSSION

When events are widely reported, mass hysteria may occur. What recent events have caused people to panic? Did media reports increase the level of panic?

Orson Welles

In the 1930s, before he became a renowned film director, Orson Welles produced radio shows. In 1938, his radio play, based on the science fiction novel *War of the Worlds*, caused panic across the United States and parts of Canada. Listen to a discussion about that historic event. Then answer the following questions.

1 Why does Fred Tudor know about this event?

_____

_____

2 Why did Fred "break in" during Welles' broadcast?

_____

_____

_____

Orson Welles

3 Describe another Welles broadcast.

_____
_____
_____
_____

4 Why did people not react in panic during this other Welles presentation?

_____
_____

5 Why didn't Fred sign off his station with a "bubbling down into quicksand" voice?

_____

6 What happened to Fred during his bicycle ride? _____

_____

7 Why did Fred get so scared during that bicycle incident? _____

_____
_____

8 According to Fred, what causes mass hysteria? _____

_____

SPEAKING

Create a Radio Play

Work with a partner or a small team of students and prepare a short "radio play" about a hoax. You could get ideas from tabloid newspapers. For example, you could present a story about a strange new species, alien messages, an invasion of killer termites, hidden cameras in televisions, and so on. Use your imagination! (To the teacher: There are more ideas in the Instructor's Manual.)

If it is appropriate for your story, you could use sound effects during your play. Remember that everyday objects are very effective for the creation of sound effects. For example, if you wear gloves and rub gravel on the ground, it sounds like a car on a road. Discover what sounds will make your production more interesting.

There are also websites that contain free sound effects. Try "Royalty-Free Sounds" at www.partnersinrhyme.com/ or go to "Soundrangers" at www.soundrangers.com/

If these sites no longer work, just go on the Net and ask for "free sound effects."

Essay Topics

Write an essay about one of the following topics. Your essay should contain an interesting introduction, two or three reasons for your opinion, and a conclusion.

1 Why do people need to believe in ghosts and spirits? What do such beliefs give us? You can quote from Bertram Rothschild's text, "The Ghost in My House." You could also think about the Hungarian proverb, "The believer is happy; the doubter is wise."

2 Prove that people are easily influenced by the media. You could refer to the Orson Welles radio drama or you could discuss more contemporary examples of panic and mass hysteria.

3 Many books and movies mix fact and fiction. (Examples: *Titanic*, *Braveheart*, *Pearl Harbour*, *JFK*, *Amistad*, etc.) How could this be dangerous?

Read about conspiracies, assassinations, UFOs, etc. at Conspiracies and Extremism. Choose your topic in the 'subject' index.
conspiracies.about.com

Check out these on-line magazines for skeptics:
The Skeptical Enquirer   www.csicop.org/si
The Skeptic Magazine   www.skeptic.org.uk

The New England Skeptical Society examines both sides of many controversial issues.
www.theness.com/encyc.html

Listen to Orson Welles' *The War of the Worlds* radio show:
www.earthstation1.com/wotw.html

This site contains all of Mercury Theater's radio programs:
www.unknown.nu/mercury

CHAPTER 3 The Greatest Players

"It is better to deserve honors and not have them than to have them and not deserve them."
— Mark Twain

Can you think of a person you honour who is not deserving of that honour? This chapter explores contemporary individuals who may, or may not, be heroic.

Admirable Individuals

Discuss the following questions with a classmate or write down your reflections in a journal.

1. Whom do people look up to and worship? Think of some individuals that many people admire. How did September 11, 2001, change our perception of heroism?
2. Whom did people probably look up to in past centuries?
3. Are there people in certain professions who get more respect, adulation, and hero worship than others? Which professions?
4. Why do we generally revere great athletes, but dismiss great thinkers as **nerds** and **geeks**?
5. Do we idolize different traits in men and in women? What traits do we generally idolize in each gender?

Learning from Our Sports Heroes

READING 3.1

In just about any country you will find people who idolize athletes. But should athletes be glorified? In the following text, Montreal-based Lisa Fitterman examines how people react when our sports idols break the law.

VOCABULARY

As you read, you will come across words in bold. In the space provided, write a synonym for that word. Use context clues!

Write definitions

EXAMPLE:
terrible

When Our Sports Idols Go On Trial

by Lisa Fitterman, The Montreal Gazette

1. They were three nice, regular guys just sitting around one morning in February, drinking coffee and watching TSN's sports highlights when one of them said something like: "Hey, why don't we go down to the courthouse and see Davey Hilton?"

2. Joel McOuat, Ben Forget and Mark Robinson, childhood buddies and now roommates in Notre Dame de Grace, were curious. They had been following the sexual-assault trial of the World Boxing Council's super middleweight champ; they read the news stories about how he is alleged to have raped two teenage girls. They studied his face, but they could not believe that he could have or would have committed such **heinous** acts.

3. "If he's guilty, it doesn't change his talent for boxing," said McOuat, who recently graduated from Concordia University and is working on a certificate in sports administration. "I'd like him to be innocent. I want to see him defend his title."

4. And so McOuat expressed what a lot of people are feeling, for many of us live and die by the prowess of athletes. When they win, we celebrate as if it was our own victory, and when they're caught cheating, we feel betrayed (remember Ben Johnson?).

5. When athletes appear in court, charged with wife-beating, rape, assault or murder, some of us close our eyes and wish that they were innocent or, at least, that the court would find them innocent. Or we go into denial.

David Hilton after a boxing match.

6. "People aren't really able to distinguish between a pop-star hero and the integrity required to be a good person," said Angela Schneider, a former Olympic rower who got her PhD in philosophy and now teaches at the International Centre for Olympics Studies at the University of Western Ontario.

7. "When a woman is a heroine, people focus on her morality and her sexuality. When it's a man, it comes down to 'Do they do their job properly? Is he being a real man?'"

8. Schneider says that fame is more important than moral character and that somehow, because an athlete is famous, he can commit crimes and people will forgive him or believe to their dying day that "he wuz framed."

9. Listen to Johnny Watson, a contractor and character witness at Hilton's trial, who traveled to Montreal from New Orleans to testify for Hilton. "In my heart and my mind,

_____ I can't believe it to be true," Watson testified. "I liked to **hang out** with him in bars. He's a celebrity [and] I'm here because there's a great injustice being done."

10 His point? How could Hilton be a rapist when he's such a famous and faithful drinking buddy?

_____ 11 Remember the infamous Black Sox scandal of 1919, when eight **grossly** underpaid Chicago White Sox players were suspended for life after they allegedly **threw** the World Series for cold hard cash. A devastated kid approached one of the players, "Shoeless" Joe Jackson, and pleaded, "Say it ain't so, Joe."

12 The parade of troubled star athletes includes such dubious luminaries as former world heavyweight champion and convicted rapist Mike Tyson and former amateur skater Tonya Harding, most recently charged with a misdemeanour after smashing her boyfriend with a hubcap.

13 Kerry Collins, now quarterback for the New York Giants, was arrested in 1998 on a drunk-driving charge while playing for the New Orleans Saints and swaggered out of the courthouse with his shirt open to his navel, unshaven. He was smirking behind a cigar. "I've been called a drunk, a racist and a loser," he said at the time. "Other than that, I'm doing fine."

_____ 14 The court **revoked** his driver's license, and the National Football League ordered him to dry out and go through rehab.

15 Super Bowl MVP Ray Lewis of the Baltimore Ravens—he of the super-large ego and super-long mink coats, who travels with a posse of ruffians—was accused of murder last year in Atlanta after traces of blood were found in his limousine.

16 The murder charges against Lewis were dropped in exchange for his testimony against his co-accused and his guilty plea to obstruction of justice for misleading investigators and instructing the ten other people in the limo to keep quiet.

17 And, of course, what would the parade be without O.J. Simpson, the most famous of all? "The Juice," a former Buffalo Bills running back turned TV broadcaster, is living testament to the fractured relationship we have with our athletes.

18 Of course, they are the exceptions in a world that has also produced role models like Wayne Gretzky and Ken Dryden, boxer Otis Grant and Jackie Robinson, who broke the colour barrier in major-league baseball and became larger than life.

19 But the bad boys make the best copy.

_____ 20 Victor Lachance of the Canadian Centre for Ethics in Sport says that the public tends to **blur** the idea of sport as a function of human excellence with sport as entertainment, pure and simple.

21 "We have constructed sport to be about human excellence, and by getting into the business of sport as entertainment, we get into the idea that it is a good show, that the participants are putting on a good show," he said from his office in Ottawa.

22 "It's not unlike the movies or the arts or theatre—do you really care that the person who produced that piece of art on your wall was stoned at the time? Do you care that the virtuoso pianist took a tranquilizer before performing Chopin?"

23 Media treatment of professional athletes has created a cult of personality, Lachance says. "It (sport) is a public trust, and when you get into the business of selling it as entertainment, you will destroy the very reason that people care about sport in the first place."

24 Back at the Montreal courthouse, a reporter stops Hilton before he leaves the courtroom: "Mr. Hilton, what do you think your responsibility is to your fans?"

25 Hilton smiles. His hair is streaked like a movie star's.

26 "I want to be a winner," he said. "I've always **strived** to be the best. This will be the fight of my life."

COMPREHENSION

1. In paragraph 11, a kid said, "Say it ain't so, Joe." **Ain't** is never used in formal English. What does *ain't* mean?

2. What technique does the author use to introduce her essay? Choose one:
   a) anecdote   b) opposite view   c) historical   d) general background

3. Is this text objective or subjective? _____
   If you answered "subjective," quote from a paragraph in which she expresses her opinion or her bias.

4. The author gives examples of many athletes who behaved badly. Beside each athlete's name, do the following:
   - Write down the type of athlete he/she is. (e.g., boxer)
   - Briefly explain what criminal act he or she committed.

   EXAMPLE: Davey Hilton   Type of athlete: *boxer*
   Criminal act: *accused of raping two teenagers*

   "Shoeless" Joe Jackson   Type of athlete: _____
   Criminal act: _____

   Tonya Harding   Type of athlete: _____
   Criminal act: _____

   Kerry Collins   Type of athlete: _____
   Criminal act: _____

   Ray Lewis   Type of athlete: _____
   Criminal act: _____

5 Quote a sentence from the text that best summarizes the author's central argument.

_____
_____

DISCUSSION / WRITTEN RESPONSE

1 In your opinion, are professional sports a demonstration of human excellence or are they entertainment? Explain your answer. Give an example to support your point of view.

2 Angela Schneider says, "When a woman is a heroine, people focus on her morality and her sexuality. When it's a man, it comes down to 'Did he do his job properly? Is he being a real man?'" Do you agree? Think of some famous women from the past century to support your view.

Are They Heroes?

Read about the following cases. With a team of students, discuss the questions that follow each scenario.

Note: Scenarios 1 and 2 are loosely based on true cases. Names have been changed.

Scenario 1

An Ontario man named Mark took his 7-year-old twins on a fishing trip. He also invited his good friend, 35-year-old Brandon. The twins wore life jackets but the two adults did not.

While the group was in the middle of the large lake, a storm hit the area and the boat overturned. The group were separated by the large waves. Mark and one daughter managed to swim to shore. The other child tried to swim, but Brandon grabbed her. Brandon, who is unable to swim well, pulled the life preserver off the seven-year-old girl. She subsequently drowned.

Brandon managed to get about 50 meters from shore when he ran out of breath. He screamed for help, and a woman who was passing by heard him. Janet, a former lifeguard, jumped into the chilly water, swam out to Brandon, and saved him.

1 Why do you think that Brandon took the 7-year-old girl's life preserver?

2 Should Brandon be punished for his act? If you answer yes, what should the criminal charge and punishment be?

3 Janet saved Brandon. Was her act heroic? Why or why not?

Scenario 2

One night, Bria, a 26-year-old single mother, put her two small children to bed. She then went to her own room. Unfortunately, she left her smoldering cigarette between the sofa cushions in the living room downstairs.

A fire started. When Bria awoke, the upstairs hallway was already filled with smoke and fire. Bria rushed to the bedroom of her two sleeping children. She managed to lower the two children out the window, and then she jumped out of the window and landed on a snowbank. Bria suffered from smoke inhalation and some minor burns. The children were not hurt.

1. Were Bria's actions heroic? Why or why not?

2. If Bria were not related to the children (for example, if she were just the babysitter), would your answer to number 5 change? Why or why not?

3. If a firefighter had saved the family, would he or she be a hero?

Scenario 3

Pablo Picasso is respected as one of the greatest artists of the twentieth century. His paintings sell for millions of dollars. Picasso was a fundamental player in many twentieth-century art movements including Cubism and Abstractionism. Some suggest that Picasso was physically abusive with many of his wives and companions. Picasso had three children whom he neglected. His oldest son claims that Pablo constantly ignored him and belittled him.

1. Many people idolize Picasso as a great artist. Is he worthy of such idolatry?

2. To what extent does his private life matter?

3. If a person does something extraordinary in a specific field (art, music, sports), is that person heroic? Why or why not?

WATCHING: The Hero Among Us

This video segment examines average people who, when confronted with a crisis, risk their lives to save others.

WATCHING COMPREHENSION

As you watch the video, answer the following questions.

1. Professor Michael Lessie studies the motives of heroes in his book titled
   a) *Rescues*   b) *The Hero Among Us*   c) *The Ultimate Courage*

2. According to Professor Lessie, what do we learn from heroes of mythology?

3 According to Professor Lessie, what do real-life heroes teach us?

_____

4 Are we all capable of heroism? Explain.

_____

_____

5 What is Major Jalbert's strategy during a crisis?
   a) Stop and think and see what you can do
   b) Act first, think later

Several heroic individuals are profiled. Write the letter of the heroic act next to the person who performed that act.

INDIVIDUAL		HEROIC ACTION
6 Anna Lang	_____	A. ran into a burning house and saved the children
7 Steve Lopez	_____	B. befriended a hijacker so that the passengers could be saved.
8 Mary Dewey	_____	C. swam through burning water to save a child.
9 David Chevarie	_____	D. jumped onto a subway track to save a suicidal woman.

10 Why would Steve Lopez not do his heroic act again?

_____

11 Professor Lessie suggests that the woman who swam through burning water was motivated by:
   a) instinct. She didn't think about it.
   b) a guilty conscience. She was the driver of the vehicle that fell off the bridge.
   c) glory. She wanted recognition for her act.

12 When the woman in the burning water yelled for help to a man on shore, the man simply ignored her. According to Professor Lessie,
   a) the man's inaction was common.
   b) the man's inaction was uncommon.

13 Why did the boy jump onto the subway tracks?
   a) He knew and trusted his own youth and fitness.
   b) He knew he could help the woman.
   c) He didn't want to spend the rest of his life thinking, "I could have done something."
   d) All of the answers

14 The stewardess chose to stay on the plane with the hijacker. Why did she make that choice?

_____

15 What happens to heroes after their feats of courage, according to Professor Lessie?

DISCUSSION OR WRITTEN RESPONSE

1 The man on the shore ignored a woman's screams for help. Why did he ignore her? What causes some people to ignore such cries for help?

2 The friends and family of the young electrical engineering student think that he should never have jumped onto the subway tracks. Remember that the film also mentions many people who died during acts of heroism. Do you think that the young man acted more recklessly than the other heroes? Explain your answer.

3 Of the five individuals mentioned in the video, which one acted in the most selfless, heroic manner? Explain your answer.

Reading Tip: Recognizing Irony

Irony is a technique that some writers use to make a point. There are three main types of irony.

Situational Irony: There is a difference between how a situation looks on the surface, and what is actually going on underneath (which can be quite the opposite).

  EXAMPLE: *A boy hears his parents whispering together. He thinks that his parents are planning a party for him. They are actually planning to divorce.*

Verbal Irony: There is a contrast between what a writer or character says and what the writer or character means.

  EXAMPLE: *A father states that it won't kill his son to study before his last exam. What the father means is that studying will be beneficial.*

Dramatic Irony: This type of irony is used in plays, stories, and novels. There is a difference between what a writer or character says or thinks about events, and what the audience or reader knows about those events.

  EXAMPLE: *A character says, "My husband has been very attentive lately. He is such a sweet person." The reader knows that the husband is actually having an affair, and he is just being nice because he feels so guilty.*

READING 3.2

Gary Lautens began a humor column and eventually published several Leacock Award-winning books including *Take My Family Please* and *No Sex Please, We're Married*. He also won a National Newspaper Award for his sports writing, which appeared in both the *Hamilton Spectator* and the *Toronto Star*. The following essay appeared in Lautens' book, *Laughing with Lautens* (1964).

In the following text, Lautens examines violence in sports. Be careful as you read. What Lautens says and what he means are not always the same thing.

VOCABULARY

As you read, you will come across words in bold. In the space provided, write a synonym for that word or expression. Use context clues!

The Greatest Player

by Gary Lautens

EXAMPLE:

meet 1 Occasionally I **run into** sports figures at cocktail parties, on the street, or on their way to the bank.

2 "Nice game the other night," I said to an old hockey-player pal.

3 "Think so?" he replied.

4 "You've come a long way since I knew you as a junior."

5 "How's that?"

_____ 6 "Well, you high-stick better for one thing-and I think the way you **clutch** sweaters is really superb. You may be the best in the league."

_____ 7 He blushed modestly. "For a time," I confessed, "I never thought you'd **get the hang of it**."

8 "It wasn't easy," he confided. "It took practice and encouragement. You know something like spearing doesn't come naturally. It has to be developed."

9 "I'm not inclined to flattery but, in my book, you've got it made. You're a dirty player."

10 "Stop kidding."

_____ 11 "No, no," I insisted. "I'm not trying to **butter you up**. I mean it. When you broke in there were flashes of dirty play—but you weren't consistent. That's the difference between a dirty player and merely a colourful one."

12 "I wish my father were alive to hear you say that," he said quietly. "He would have been proud."

13 "Well, it's true. There isn't a player in the league who knows as many obscene gestures."

14 "I admit I have been given a few increases in pay in recent years. Management seems to be treating me with new respect."

_____ 15 "You're selling tickets," I said. "You're a **gate attraction** now—not some bum who only can skate and shoot and the rest of it. Your profanity is beautiful."

16 "C'mon."

17 "No, I'm serious. I don't think anyone in the league can incite a riot the way you can."

18 "I've had a lot of help along the way. You can't make it alone," he stated generously.

19 "No one does," I said.

20 "Take that play where I skate up to the referee and stand nose-to-nose with my face turning red. It was my junior coach who taught me that. He was the one who used to toss all the sticks on the ice and throw his hat into the stands and pound his fist on the boards."

21 "You were lucky to get that sort of training. A lot of players never learn the fundamentals."

22 "I think there are a few boys in the league who can spit better than me."

23 "Farther, perhaps, but not more accurately," I corrected.

24 "Well, thanks anyway. I've always considered it one of my weaknesses."

25 "That last **brawl** of yours was perfectly executed. Your sweater was torn off, you taunted the crowd, you smashed your stick across the goal posts."

26 "The papers gave me a break. The coverage was outstanding."

27 "Do you ever look back to the days when you couldn't cut a forehead or puff a lip or insult an official?"

28 "Everyone gets nostalgic," he confessed. "It's a good thing I got away from home by the time I was fifteen. I might never have been any more than a ham-and-egger, you know, a twenty-goal man who drifts through life unnoticed."

29 "What was the turning point?"

30 "I had heard prominent sportsmen say that nice guys finish last, and that you have to beat them in the alley if you hope to beat them in the rink. But it didn't sink in."

31 "Nobody learns overnight."

32 "I wasted a few years learning to play my wing and to check without using the butt of the stick. But I noticed I was being passed by. I skated summers to keep in shape, exercised, kept curfew."

33 "Don't tell me. They said you were **dull**."

34 "Worse than that. They said I was clean. It's tough to live down that sort of reputation."

35 I nodded.

36 "Anyway, during a game in the sticks, I was skating off the ice—we had won five-one and I had scored three goals. The home crowd was pretty listless and there was some booing. Then it happened."

37 "What?"

38 "My big break. My mother was in the stands and she shouted to me. I turned to wave at her with my hockey stick and I accidentally caught the referee across the face. He bled a lot—took ten stitches later."

39 "Is that all?"

40 "Well, someone pushed me and I lost my balance and fell on the poor man. A real brawl started. Luckily, I got credit for the whole thing—went to jail overnight, got a suspension. And, talk about fate! A big league scout was in the arena. He offered me a contract right away."

41 "It's quite a success story," I said.

42 "You've got to get the breaks," he replied, humbly.

COMPREHENSION

1 How are the following parts of the text ironic?
For example, the title.
When Lautens calls the athlete the "greatest" player, he actually means that the athlete is the "dirtiest" player.

- paragraph 8 _____
  _____

- paragraphs 20, 21 _____
  _____

- paragraph 34 _____
  _____

- paragraph 41 _____
  _____

2 How is the dirty player's "big break" ironic? (See paragraphs 36 to 40.)
_____
_____

3 Lautens blames several groups of people for sports violence. For example, he blames the audience. In paragraph 15 he writes, "You're selling tickets … you're a gate attraction now."
Find two other sports-related groups that he blames, and provide one supporting quotation for each group.

i) _____
_____

ii) _____
_____

4 What is Lautens' main point?
_____
_____

5 Lautens uses humour (satire) to make his point. Would this text have been more effective if he had written a traditional persuasive essay about sports violence? Explain your view.
_____
_____

DISCUSSION / WRITTEN RESPONSE

1. Some believe that violent contact sports mimic the battlefield. Do you agree?

2. This text was written in 1964. Could Lautens be writing about contemporary hockey players? Is it true that violence in sports is still necessary to attract the fans? Why is that?

Murder on Ice

Many people think the hockey rink is no place for police or the courts. That argument came under scrutiny in the late 1990s. Vancouver police launched an investigation after a Boston Bruins defenceman struck an opposing player in the head with a vicious swing of his stick. The issue is hardly new. Listen to a true story about an early case of hockey violence.

Pre-Listening Vocabulary

Before you listen, ensure that you understand the following terms:

- Trial
- Crown Prosecutor
- Defendant
- Sentence
- Witnesses
- Manslaughter
- Death by hanging
- Rough play

COMPREHENSION

Answer the following questions on a separate piece of paper.

1. Who are the following people?
   a. Alcide Laurin
   b. Alan Loney
   c. F. J. French
   d. Robert Pringle

2. Summarize what happened in the story. Include the following elements in your summary.
   - When did the events happen?
   - What teams were involved in the case?
   - What happened to Laurin and Loney?
   - Why did the courts respond as they did?

(To the teacher: More detailed questions appear in the instructor's manual.)

DISCUSSION

1. How would the courts respond today if a similar case of hockey violence occurred?

2. Should violence that occurs in team sports be treated differently than violence that occurs in public places, on the road, or in the home? Why or why not?

Essay Topics

Write a 300- to 400-word essay about one of the topics below.

Your essay should have

- a compelling introduction that includes one of the following thesis statements in its original or modified form.
- two or three reasons for your opinion
- a conclusion that brings your essay to a satisfactory close.

1. Famous actors (or musicians or athletes) are (or are not) good role models.
2. There are three qualities that make a person heroic.
3. The individual from the last century who is most likely to be remembered and mythologized is . . .

This site has information on some 20th-century heroes:
www.drake.edu/journalism/CenturysEnd/heroes.html

Reflections on twentieth-century heroes:
www.heroism.org/class/1980/scholar.htm

You can read biographies about many cultural icons at the following biography websites:
www.biography.com

Warning:
Sometimes Internet sites move or are discontinued. If the previous web addresses are no longer available, just go to a search engine and type in key words about your topic.

CHAPTER 4 Conscience

We are each burdened with prejudice; against the poor or the rich, the smart or the slow, the gaunt or the obese. It is natural to develop prejudices. It is noble to rise above them.
— Source Unknown

Think about this quotation. Do you think that you have "risen above" your own prejudices? In this chapter you will be asked to explore the roots of racism.

Cultural Connections

Discuss the following questions with your classmates.

1. What makes people become prejudiced against certain groups or cultures?
2. Do you think that one day a "global culture" could exist without prejudice? Has it already begun to appear?
3. Read the quotation at the beginning of this chapter. Do you agree that "it is natural to develop prejudices?"
4. How can people *unlearn* prejudices?

Columbus, Hero or Villain

In 1992, America celebrated the 500th anniversary of Christopher Columbus's arrival in the New World. Many native groups protested the glorification of a man who initiated the destruction of lives and cultures. Supporters of Columbus feel that his achievements should continue to be recognized and celebrated. This video re-examines Columbus's legacy.

TEAM DISCUSSION

Watch the video and discuss the following questions with two or three other students. Write your group's answers in the spaces provided.

1. How large was the native population in North America when Columbus arrived?

2 In the century that followed Columbus's arrival in the New World, the native population shrunk by about how many people?

_____

3 What caused the deaths among the natives?

_____
_____

4 Why do many groups believe that Columbus Day should not be celebrated?

_____
_____
_____
_____

5 According to Dawn Ruby, a University of Toronto historian, Columbus "didn't set off as a conqueror. He merely took an important series of voyages that had effects both good and bad. To blame him personally is way out of proportion." Do you agree? Explain your answer.

_____
_____
_____
_____

DISCUSSION

According to current historical thinking, who was the first European (after the Vikings) to set foot on Canadian soil? If you are Canadian and you don't know the answer, then why do you think Canadians do not celebrate this event? Are Canadians any less prone to mythmaking than Americans? Explain your answer.

Reading Tip:
Determine the Author's Purpose

As you read, ask yourself why the author wrote the text. Most texts are written for one of the following reasons:

1. to entertain → The author hopes to get an emotional response from the reader. The text may evoke laughter, tears, anger, frustration, shock, etc.
2. to inspire → The author hopes to leave the reader inspired.
3. to persuade → The author expresses an opinion and hopes to influence the reader.
4. to inform → The author presents information about a topic. The author tries to remain neutral and does not intend to persuade the reader.

When you read, ask yourself, "What is the author's *main* intention?"

PAIR READING ACTIVITY (optional)

Find a partner. One of you could read "Racism's Source," and the other could read "P is for Prejudice." Only answer the questions that follow your reading. You could answer the questions with a team of students who have read the same text as you.

Later, you will find a partner who has read the other text and you will share information with him or her.

READING 4.1

Gwynne Dyer is a native of Newfoundland, Canada. He is currently a London-based independent journalist whose articles are published in 45 countries. In the following essay, Dyer examines the roots of racism.

Racism's Source

by Gwynne Dyer

1. "What are you doing here in Germany," asked the three drunken youths when they ran into Alberto Adriano in Dessau one Saturday night in June. "I live here," Adriano might have replied, but he didn't get the chance. Enrico Hilprecht, 24, and Frank Miethbauer and Christian Richter, both 16, were still rhythmically kicking and stamping on his head with their steel-capped boots and chanting "Get out of our country, you n _ _ _ _ _ pig" when the police pulled up and arrested them.

2. Adriano's skinhead killers went on trial with Germany's chief federal prosecutor, Kay Nehm, personally leading the prosecution. Hilprecht was sent to prison for life, and the two teenagers were each given nine-year sentences.

3. Germany is considering a ban on the neo-Nazi National Party of Germany, whose members are involved in a high proportion of attacks on racial minorities.

4. These responses would be more reassuring, however, if the xenophobia were confined to a few neo-fascists. It isn't; it's a popular sport throughout eastern Germany.

5. So is there some special wickedness in the Germans that makes them instinctive racists, in Hitler's time or in our own? One doubts that Christian Richardson would think so.

6. Richardson is English, and moved to Dublin last year to be with his 24-year-old Irish girlfriend. He quickly found a good job in the booming Irish capital, and last June his parents came over from England to visit him. His father is white and his mother is black, which would not have turned any heads in his native city of Bristol. In Dublin, it nearly got them killed.

7. Walking back from a restaurant right in the center of Dublin, the three were set upon by white Irish youths. Christian Richardson's father was stabbed six times in the neck and back as he tried to protect his Jamaican-born wife. He almost died.

8. His son treated it as an isolated incident and stayed in Dublin—until it happened again in mid-August as he was bicycling to work. "It was broad daylight," said Richardson. "Three lads shouted a load of racist abuse at me as I passed them, and then started coming after me. I was terrified. I thought: "That's it. I'm off. No way I'm staying around to take this." I just packed my bag and got on a plane."

9. There is racist violence in England, too, but Richardson clearly feels a lot safer in England than in Ireland. As for eastern Germany, it is off the scale: racial attacks there are four times more frequent than in Britain. So what did East Germany and Ireland have in common that could account for their brutal racism? Not much, on the face of it.

10. Ireland is Catholic; eastern Germany is Protestant. Ireland was a British colony; Eastern Germany (as Prussia) was a great power. Germany is one of the poorest regions of the European Union with unemployment of over more than 17 percent; Ireland is now the "Celtic Tiger" with an economy growing three times faster than the European average and only four percent unemployment.

11. But there is one common factor. These are both places where almost everybody was white until recently. Perhaps the problem is not innate, ineradicable racism, but just the panicky reaction of an isolated population when its ethnic homogeneity and cultural conformity begins to be challenged.

12. German politicians (and now some Irish ones too) respond to outbreaks of racial violence with demands for tighter immigration controls, as if the problem were too many foreigners. But there is a strong case for saying that the real problem is too few.

13. Compare Britain, which has had large-scale immigration for over a generation and is now a fairly relaxed multi-racial society, to Ireland, a society only recently emerged from the Catholic nationalist dream of a single people united by religion, language, and history. Or compare former West Germany, which has taken in lots of immigrants since the 1960s, to former Communist East Germany, which spent 40 years living in a cave.

14. The lowest rate of racist violence in Germany is in the state of Saarland, on the French border, where 8.2 percent of the population is foreign-born. The highest rate is in Saxony-Anhalt, where only 1.7 percent are foreigners, and an even tinier proportion are non-white. All the other eastern states share the same pattern of high anti-foreign violence and practically no foreigners.

15. So maybe the real solution is to flood the place with people from elsewhere, and wait for the locals to get used to diversity. Of course, first you have to figure out some way to persuade the outsiders to stay.

COMPREHENSION

(Option: Answer these questions with a group of students who have read the same text.)

Looking for Details

1 How do Ireland and East Germany compare? Fill in the following chart.

	IRELAND	EAST GERMANY
Religion		
Wealth and Economy		
Employment Rate		
General race of population until recently		

For numbers 2 to 4, indicate whether the statements are true or false according to the text. Circle *T* (for "true") or *F* (for "false"). If the sentence is false, write down the true information.

2 Alberto Adriano said, "I live here" to his attackers.   T   F

_____

3 Richardson left Ireland because he felt unsafe.   T   F

_____

4 Poverty and unemployment are the main factors in racist attacks.   T   F

_____

5 The author, Gwynne Dyer, believes that there is a "special wickedness" in Germans.   T   F

_____

Finding the Central Purpose and Central Argument

6 What introduction style does the author use? _____

7 Although the author does several things in this text, he has one central purpose. What is the author's purpose? Choose one of the following.

  a) to entertain   **b)** to inspire   **c)** to persuade   **d)** to inform

8 Is the text objective or subjective? _____

If you answered subjective, quote from a paragraph in which the author expresses his opinion or his bias.

_____

9 The author begins by giving examples and then builds towards his central argument. What is the author's central argument?

_____

_____

10 How can we get rid of racism, according to Dyer?

___

READING 4.2

Toronto-based Allen Abel has held positions as varied as Beijing bureau chief of the Toronto *Globe and Mail*, science columnist for *Saturday Night* magazine, and feature interviewer for CBC-TV's *Hockey Night in Canada*. From 1986 to 1995, Allen was the on-air host, writer, and co-producer of more than 100 prime-time documentaries for CBC-TV's current-affairs program *The Journal*. In the following essay, Abel examines the work of Dr. Frances Aboud.

P is for Prejudice

by Allen Abel

1. A five-year-old girl we'll call Danielle crosses the hallway from her kindergarten class to a tiny meeting room at a public school in central Montreal. Waiting for her are McGill University professor of psychology Frances Aboud and one of her graduate students.

2. Dr. Aboud has brought a binder of pictures for Danielle to consider. The illustrations are simple drawings of boys and girls, men and women, two to each page, each pair identical except for the colour of their skin and the texture of their hair. Each page is linked to a question, which the graduate student reads to the little girl.

3. *Some boys are mean. When they come home from school, and their dog comes to meet them, they kick their dog. Who is mean?*

4. Danielle points to the brown-skinned boy.

5. The testing goes on: *Some boys are clean … Some girls are not good-looking … Some boys are kind … Some boys are nice … Some girls won't let others play … Some men don't share. Who won't share?*

6. Five times out of six, Danielle, who is white, selects the white character for a positive attribute. And five times out of six, she chooses the black subject as the negative.

7. It is easy to suspect that she answers in this way because her parents have sown the seeds of hate within her, or because she is living in a racist world. Perhaps her teacher has failed, or television has tainted her mind. But Dr. Aboud believes that little Danielle is prejudiced because she is developing normally, and because she is five years old. Discrimination was wired into her brain at conception—as it is into my brain, and yours.

8. "Prejudice is biological," the professor says. It is a powerful statement on which she has staked her academic reputation.

9. At McGill since 1975, Dr. Aboud has specialized in childhood racial awareness, testing thousands of children as young as three with picture books and flash cards to calibrate —and perhaps someday to cure—the impulse that may be inborn.

10 "Any parent knows that when you walk down the street with a two-year-old, they comment on the colour of people," she says. 'There's a pink lady; there's a brown lady.' At that age, they just see colour."

11 "At about the age of four or five, they begin to realize that skin colour is a constancy and it's attached to you. It kicks in that they are part of a group, and they prefer people whom they can identify as part of their group. Many things are important clues in figuring out who belongs to which group, but skin colour and hair texture are the two big ones. This is where prejudice comes in."

12 Dr. Aboud says that at five years of age, about 50 to 60 percent of children have negative "out-group" feelings, which is to say that they distrust anyone outside their own group. "It's not that they don't like the other groups, but they prefer their own," she says. "It's not hatred of the others — it's suspicion of differences."

13 At age four or five, Dr. Aboud notes, children do not have the verbal skills to express their racial attitudes, and parents who are careful not to discuss racial issues in the home are often shocked to learn that their kids have registered as prejudiced on her "Who is mean?" tests.

14 "I tell the parents, 'It doesn't come from you.' So they blame the school — they think it has to come from *somewhere*. I tell them that it doesn't come from school, either.

15 "So they think we cause it by doing our tests."

16 Nearly everything in our political and popular culture argues that Frances Aboud must be wrong. The French novelist and poet Tahar Ben Jelloun affirms it in *Racism Explained to My Daughter*: "No one is born racist. If your parents or the people around you don't put racist ideas into your head, there's no reason you should become so."

17 Psychologist William Bukowski at Concordia University is convinced that Frances Aboud is getting it right. "What she has shown is that children of a certain age are *all* prejudiced, regardless of what views their parents have," Dr. Bukowski tells me. "Prejudice gives you a very simple way of seeing the world. Life is complex — and when you're a child, you've just begun to see that complexity. The desire for simplicity is a human frailty, and that is translated in a child's mind into a preference for in-group members."

18 If little Danielle continues along the normal path of human cognitive development, her preference for people with her skin colour and hair type over "different" people will intensify until she is seven, then diminish measurably.

19 "Eight is the age of reason," says Frances Aboud. "They come out of their egocentric state and realize that there are other perspectives: whites can be both positive and negative; blacks can be both positive and negative. The same kids, when we test them at five, they're prejudiced, and when we test them again at nine, they're not."

20 "The question is, why do some kids remain prejudiced?" says Professor Anna Beth Doyle of Concordia, Dr. Aboud's long-time collaborator. "What we need to find out next is what happens to some kids that they *don't* continue to [remain racist], and to some kids that they *do*."

21 Twenty-five years of research have taught Frances Aboud what works in building tolerance, and what doesn't. What does not work, she says, is the nominal mixing of the tribes. "It's not just integrating the schools, where you put them together," she says. "You have to have them in the same class, intensively working on projects in mixed pairs or in mixed groups. Having a succession of cross-race friends—friends you respect and trust—has a positive impact later on. But it's got to be more than one [friend], and it's got to be at the level of real co-operative learning and working together."

22 "Prejudice *can* be changed," she says, "but you've got to overdo it—you've got to be explicit about it. You have to talk specifically about bias, and how to intervene to stop it."

COMPREHENSION

(Option: Answer these questions with a group of students who have read the same text.)

1 What are Dr. Aboud's conclusions about the stages of development and prejudice?

	RACIST TENDENCIES, ATTITUDES, BELIEFS
Age 2	
Age 4-5	
Age 8-9	

For numbers 2 to 5, decide whether the statements are true or false according to Dr. Aboud. Write *T* (for "true") or *F* (for "false") after each statement. If the sentence is false, write down the true information.

2 Parents and a racist society are to blame when children are racist.   T   F

_____

3 Children pass through a stage where they have prejudice tendencies.   T   F

_____

4 About 50% of five-year-olds hate people from other racial groups.   T   F

_____

5 If children go to mixed-race schools, they will lose their racist tendencies.   T   F

_____

6 What is the point of Dr. Aboud's research?

_____

7 Although the author does several things in this text, he has one central purpose. What is the author's purpose? Choose one of the following.

a) to entertain   b) to inspire   c) to persuade   d) to inform

8 Is the text objective or subjective? _____

If you answered subjective, quote from a paragraph in which the author expresses his opinion or his bias.

_____

9 According to Dr. Aboud, how can we build a less-racist society?

_____
_____

PAIR READING: SHARE YOUR INFORMATION

Compare "Racism's Source" and "P is for Prejudice." Sit with someone who has read the other text. Share general information about your text with your partner by answering the following questions.

1 What causes prejudice?

Gwynne Dyer	Dr. Aboud

2 How does each person prove his or her point?

Gwynne Dyer	Dr. Aboud

3 What is Dyer or Aboud's opinion on how to build a less prejudiced society?

Gwynne Dyer	Dr. Aboud

Discuss the next two questions.

1. How do Dyer and Aboud contradict each other?
2. Which argument makes more sense? Why?

Pakistan

Calgary freelancer Aziza Sindhu travelled to her parents' home in Pakistan to explore her culture and heritage. She discovered much more than she bargained for. Listen to the interview with Aziza and answer the questions that follow.

1. Give background information on Aziza Sindhu.

   a) How old is she? _____

   b) Has she been to Pakistan before this trip? When? _____

   c) How did she feel about her Pakistani roots growing up in Calgary?

2. In Pakistan, Aziza's half-brother Seemab became her tour guide. Aziza tells Seemab about her lifestyle in Canada. Describe her lifestyle.

3. What is Seemab's opinion of Aziza's lifestyle in Canada?

4. How did Aziza escape her parents' desire to set her up in an arranged marriage?

5. Aziza uncovers Seemab's hypocrisy. What does she discover?

6. What advice does Aziza give Seemab about his marriage?

7. What secret does Aziza discover about her father?

8 What "price" did Seemab pay in order to keep his natural father in his life?

_____

_____

9 What do Aziza and Seemab discover that they have in common?

_____

Developing Strong Arguments

In higher education, you are often called upon to develop and defend your point of view. Why is the ability to argue effectively so important?

In fact, we incorporate argument in every aspect of our lives, both personal and professional. When you debate which university to attend, which career to choose, or which movie to watch, you communicate your choice based on a logical analysis of the alternatives. In most professions you are called upon to state and defend your views.

PREPARING FOR ARGUMENTS

When you have to make a presentation about an issue, think the issue through carefully. Note down important arguments for both sides of the issue. If you must debate an issue with others, it is important that you be able to predict your opponents' arguments.

Supporting Your View

Find support for your views from reliable sources. You could use the following types of evidence:

a) Tell a true story

Gwynne Dyer used true news stories to support his thesis in the text, "Racism's Source." You could also use true anecdotes from your life to support your point of view.

b) Make an analogy

Compare the opposite view to something absurd. For example, if you argue against a smoking ban, you could claim that "banning smoking is like banning bad breath, because bad breath disturbs the environment of others."

c) Quote respected sources

Someone who has studied the issue could be considered a respectable source. If you quote a source in written or spoken presentations, explain who the source is.

d) Show long-term consequences

Every solution to a problem can carry long-term consequences with it. For example, in response to the terrorist attacks of September 11, 2001, many governments enacted anti-terrorism legislation. However, in some cases the new laws may be used to suppress legitimate dissent or free speech. And the new laws could be misused or misinterpreted by future governments.

e) Use emotional argument

The strongest arguments can be emotional ones. Sometimes the most effective way to influence others is to appeal to their sense of justice, humanity, pride, and even guilt.

However, do not rely only on emotional arguments! And do not mistake an appeal to emotion with an appeal to base instincts. If you use emotionally charged words (for example, if you call someone *ignorant*) or if you make broad generalizations about racial, ethnic, linguistic, or religious groups, you will seriously undermine your argument.

Speaking Activity

MILITARY COURT CASE

You now have a chance to practice debating an issue. Imagine that you are part of a military tribunal. You must determine whether Corporal Hanes should be jailed for murder.

Read the case below together with your teacher. Identify any terms that are unfamiliar. Your teacher will divide the class into two teams. One team must argue that Hanes is innocent and the other team must argue that he is guilty. Your team will have about ten minutes to prepare your argument. You will then have the opportunity to debate the case with the other half of the class.

The Corporal Hanes Case

Background

On March 4, 1999, at 5:20 AM, near the city of Bangui in the Philippines, two unarmed civilians, Fernand Ramin and his son Rafael, were shot and killed. They were inside a military compound. There is evidence that they cut through a chain link fence. Both bodies were found near a military building containing electronic goods.

Fernand was shot three times in the chest. Rafael was shot once in the side of the head and twice in the back. Corporal Gregory Hanes shot both men.

There had been one previous break-in at the military base. One month earlier, on February 6, a military building containing electronic goods had been broken into. Radios and electronic parts had been stolen and the thieves had escaped. The soldier who was on guard duty that night was subsequently reprimanded because he hadn't properly protected the compound.

After the second break-in, General Pino ordered that soldiers use force should they discover any intruders in the compound. Corporal Hanes was asked to do guard duty on March 4.

The Shooting

Hanes began his guard duty at 11 PM on March 3. The shooting occurred at 5:20 the next morning. At the time of the shooting, the sun was rising and there was some light and some shadow.

Hanes claims that the civilians were about 20 feet from him. Later military patrols measured the distance, and estimated that the civilians and soldier must have been no more than 10 feet apart at the time of the shooting.

Corporal Hanes stated that he ordered the civilians to raise their arms and surrender, but that the civilians started to walk towards him. Hanes claims that he repeated, "Raise your arms" in a clear, loud voice. Hanes stated that he feared for his life.

Next to the site of the shooting, about 18 feet away, stands a sleeping barracks. Twenty-two soldiers were asleep at the time of the shooting. The sleeping soldiers heard nothing but six gunshots.

The Suspect

Corporal Hanes was part of a racist skinhead group during his youth. When he was seventeen, he served six months in juvenile detention for a vicious attack on an immigrant.

Now twenty-five-year-old Corporal Hanes is a decorated soldier and he has one medal for bravery: during a previous tour of duty in Somalia, he saved a fellow soldier after a land-mine explosion.

Corporal Hanes claims he was following orders. Electronic equipment had gone missing. Orders were to use force if the soldiers discovered someone breaking into the compound. Corporal Hanes claims that he was never reprimanded after the incident.

The Victims

The dead man, Fernand Ramin, had seven children. According to his wife, he was distraught about the weak conditions of his two youngest daughters who were malnourished. Mr. Ramin and his oldest son were only trying to get food, according to his family.

At the time of his death, 39-year-old Fernand Ramin was 5 foot 7, and he weighed 119 pounds. His 14-year-old son Rafael was 5 foot 4, and weighed 99 pounds.

Mr. Fernand Ramin was wearing baggy pants and a sleeveless shirt at the time of his death. He had nothing in his hands, and his pockets were empty except for a pair of pliers found in his back pocket. His son Rafael had on a T-shirt and loose pants. Rafael's hands and pockets were empty.

Both Fernand and Rafael Ramin speak Tagalog only. The soldier speaks English and French.

Upon a search of Mr. Ramin's home, no electronic goods were found. There was no evidence that the family was profiting financially from any illegal activity.

Testimony from Other Soldiers

Photos suggest that Corporal Hanes is still part of a racist group. In one photo taken six months before the shooting, Hanes is standing with a group of people near a swastika. Several witnesses have testified that Corporal Hanes often makes racist jokes and comments about the Filipino people.

Private Barnes has testified that Corporal Hanes often bragged about the killings. Private Barnes has confided that he thinks the two civilians were murdered. He was in the nearby barracks, and he says that he wasn't completely asleep at the time of the killings. He says that he didn't hear any shouting or any warnings; he only heard the gunshots.

Other Evidence

On March 15, 1996, Gregory Hanes was made a corporal. Some of the other soldiers resented his increase in rank. One soldier in particular, Private Barnes, stated his unhappiness to other soldiers. Private Barnes was quoted as saying that he has more experience and is more level-headed than Gregory Hanes, and Barnes believed that he, instead of Hanes, should have gotten the increase in rank.

During their tour of duty in the Philippines, all of the soldiers in the unit, including Corporal Hanes, were taking the anti-malarial drug mefloquine. There is evidence that the drug may have possible side effects including nausea, nightmares, and paranoia.

Local Pressure

Pressure from the local community has been applied to the military unit. According to the mayor from the city of Bangui, a poor and hungry unarmed man and his son were slaughtered. Local townspeople believe that even if the Ramins were intending to steal something, they didn't deserve to be shot. On the steps of the mayor's office, Mrs. Ramin often sits, sobbing: "I lost my husband and son."

■ Should Corporal Hanes be convicted of murder at a military tribunal?

Argue for or against his guilt. In this trial, Hanes can be found guilty if there is a preponderance of evidence that points to his guilt.

Work with a team of students to plan your arguments. Highlight any evidence that helps your position.

Imagine what the other team might say and prepare counter-arguments.

Speaking Presentation

DEBATE OR PRESENT A CONTROVERSIAL ISSUE

Debate another student about a controversial issue, or simply present your point of view about a current controversy. If you have trouble coming up with ideas, there are lists of controversial issues in the appendix. You could also choose one of the "fact or fantasy" topics that appear at the beginning of Chapter 2.

Structure your arguments

1. Introduce your topic. In speaking presentations, just as in essay writing, it is important to make an appealing introduction. You might begin with an interesting and relevant quotation, with an anecdote, or with historical or general background information. Then state your central point in one sentence.

2. Present your reasons for your opinion. You might work specifically on three arguments. For each point, find one or more of the following:
   - statistical evidence
   - anecdotal evidence
   - informed opinions

   You will have to do some research. You could look for information on the Internet, in newspapers, magazines, or in libraries. You could also ask knowledgeable and informed people about the issue.

3. Conclude your presentation. Remind your audience of your main points. End with a suggestion or prediction.

READING 4.3

Italo Calvino was born in Santiago de las Vegas, Cuba, of Italian parents. As a youth, he moved with his family to Italy. During the World War II he was drafted into the Young Fascists, but he left and sought refuge in the Alps.

In the following text, translated by Tim Parks, Italo Calvino brilliantly questions the whole premise behind wars.

Conscience

by Italo Calvino

Came a war and a guy called Luigi asked if he could go, as a volunteer.

Everyone was full of praise. Luigi went to the place where they were handing out the rifles, took one and said: "Now I'm going to go and kill a guy called Alberto."

They asked him who Alberto was.

"An enemy," he answered, "an enemy of mine."

They explained to him that he was supposed to be killing enemies of a certain type, not whoever he felt like.

"So?" said Luigi. "You think I'm dumb? This Alberto is precisely that type. One of them. When I heard you were going to war against that lot, I thought: I'll go too, that way I can kill Alberto. That's why I came. I know that Alberto: he's a crook. He betrayed me, for next to nothing he made me make a fool of myself with a woman. It's an old story. If you don't believe me, I'll tell you the whole thing."

They said fine, it was okay.

"Right," said Luigi, "then tell me where Alberto is and I'll go there and I'll fight."

They said they didn't know.

"Doesn't matter," Luigi said. "I'll find someone to tell me. Sooner or later I'll catch up with him."

They said he couldn't do that, he had to go and fight where they sent him, and kill whoever happened to be there. They didn't know anything about this Alberto.

20 "You see," Luigi insisted, "I really will have to tell you the story. Because that guy is a real crook and you're doing the right thing going to fight against him."

But the others didn't want to know.

Luigi couldn't see reason: "Sorry, it may be all the same to you if I kill one enemy or another, but I'd be upset if I killed someone who had nothing to do with Alberto."

The others lost their patience. One of them gave him a good talking to and explained what war was all about and how you couldn't go and kill the particular enemy you wanted to.

Luigi shrugged. "If that's how it is," he said, "you can count me out."

"You're in and you're staying in," they shouted.

30 "Forward march, one-two, one-two!" And they sent him off to war.

Luigi wasn't happy. He'd kill people, offhand, just to see if he might get Alberto, or one of his family. They gave him a medal for every enemy he killed, but he wasn't happy. "If I don't kill Alberto," he thought, "I'll have killed a load of people for nothing." And he felt bad.

In the meantime they were giving him one medal after another, silver, gold, everything.

Luigi thought: "Kill some today, kill some tomorrow, there'll be less of them. That crook's bound to come."

But the enemy surrendered before Luigi could find Alberto. He felt bad he'd killed so many people for nothing, and since they were at peace now he put all his medals in a bag
40 and went around the enemy country giving them away to the wives and children of the dead.

Going around like this, he ran into Alberto.

"Good," he said, "better late than never," and he killed him.

That was when they arrested him, tried him for murder and hanged him. At the trial he said over and over that he had done it to settle his conscience, but nobody listened to him.

WRITTEN COMPREHENSION

Write or type your answers on a separate piece of paper.

1 In 6 to 8 sentences, summarize what happened.

2 Why does Luigi want to kill Alberto? Does Luigi have a good reason for wanting to kill Alberto? Explain your answer.

3 Explain Luigi's moral code. According to Luigi, who deserves to be killed and who doesn't?

④ Explain the army's moral code. Who deserves to be killed and who doesn't?

⑤ At the end of the story, Luigi is hanged. How is this ending absurd?

⑥ Calvino doesn't directly state his main point. You have to infer (or guess) what his main point is by looking for clues and then making a deduction. In your opinion, what is Calvino's main point? What message is he trying to relate?

⑦ How is Calvino's message relevant today?

Essay Topics

Choose one of the following topics and write an essay.

① John Bemrose, in a recent *Maclean's* article titled "Rails of Reconciliation," makes the following statement:

"If history teaches anything, it's that there's no such thing as a pure culture. All cultures are the product of earlier cultures mixing, changing each other, producing something new."

Do you disagree with Bemrose's statement? Do you believe that your family has a pure, distinct culture? If so, what three things differentiate your family's culture from that of other societies?

Do you agree with Bemrose's statement? If so, explain how cultures are currently overlapping in your society. How has your community's culture been influenced by other cultures around you?

② What causes wars? Think of three reasons that countries engage in wars.

Artists against racism:
www.artistsagainstracism.com

The first two articles presented in this chapter appeared in Canadian magazines. You can read more magazine articles on the Net:

Atlantic Monthly Magazine
www.theatlantic.com

Maclean's Magazine
www.macleans.ca

This site contains the addresses of many on-line magazines. You can read magazines devoted to travel, health, sports, science, culture, etc.
www.newsdirectory.com

Chapter 4

CHAPTER 5 Innocence

Anybody who has survived his childhood has enough information about life to last him the rest of his days.
— Flannery O'Connor

Childhood is traditionally considered a time of innocence. But are children so naive? This chapter examines that early stage of life.

Team Discussions

When you write essays or do speaking presentations, you are asked to present your thesis and supporting arguments. This warm-up activity will provide you with the opportunity to practice developing thesis statements and supporting arguments.

Your teacher will place you in small groups. Each group will focus on one topic.

Do the following:

- Read the text.
- Discuss the questions related to the topic.
- Write down your team's opinion in the form of a thesis statement.
- Come up with three supporting ideas for your thesis statement. Use transitional expressions to link your supporting arguments.

For example:

> **Topic: Swearing**
> Maria's twelve-year-old son has begun to use the "f" word around the house. She is getting fed up and is considering a total ban on all movies that contain swearing. She also plans to punish her son each time he swears.
>
> - Is this a justified response? Should children who swear be punished?
> - Should she just accept that swearing is a harmless way for children to rebel?
>
> Write a statement of opinion (thesis statement) about the issue.
>
> Here is a possible thesis statement:
> *It is not a serious problem if a child sometimes swears.*

> Here are possible supporting arguments:
> 1) *Swear words are simply culturally unacceptable terms that could change over time.*
> 2) *Moreover, children need ways to express their rebelliousness and swearing is a rather harmless way to do that.*
> 3) *Finally, most teenagers outgrow their "swearing" stage as they get older and become more articulate.*

Now begin.

TEAM A   Topic: Sperm Donor Children

Kelley Vieira, a 19-year-old Vancouver woman, was conceived by the use of artificial insemination: her father was a sperm donor. Kelley's mother wanted to have a baby but no husband.

Kelley wants to meet her biological father. She is part of a movement of donor-inseminated children who want the same legal rights as adopted children. They want to know about their donor's medical history. They also worry that they might marry and fall in love with a half-sibling. And Kelley wants to meet her biological dad. "I really need to know my father. My life is incomplete without him," Kelley says.

- Generally sperm donors don't expect to meet their "children." Should their identification and records be available to their offspring?
- Some sperm donors may have seventy or eighty other children. What problems could happen if sperm donor records are unsealed?
- What are some positive things about new reproductive technologies? What are some negative things?

Write a statement of opinion (thesis statement) about the issue.

_____
_____
_____

Write three supporting arguments:

1. _____
   _____

2. _____
   _____

3. _____
   _____

TEAM B   Topic: Divorce

John and Melanie got married nine years ago and they have two daughters. A few months ago, John left his wife. He moved into an apartment with his girlfriend and he wants custody of the children.

Melanie thinks that John is a poor role model for her daughters because he is an adulterer.

Also, she cannot afford to stay in Toronto, and she would like to move to Vancouver to be near her parents. Now they are having a huge court battle and the children are very upset.

- Should children be allowed to choose which parent they live with? If so, at what age?
- Should there be a law that forbids parents from moving to another city after a divorce? In other words, should both parents be forced to stay near the child?
- What can parents do to limit the trauma that divorce could cause children?

Write a statement of opinion (thesis statement) about the issue.

_____
_____
_____

Write three supporting arguments:

1. _____
   _____

2. _____
   _____

3. _____
   _____

TEAM C   Topic: Discipline

Fernando and Maggie have a good marriage. They have a twin boys, aged 9. Fernando is a very good father but he is also quite strict. When the boys are unruly, Fernando spanks them.

Fernando argues that he was spanked as a child, and it never hurt him. He also feels that when children are spanked on the bum, they do not really get hurt. He points out that he never hits the children on any other part of the body. Maggie thinks that they should find another way to punish the children.

- Are there circumstances for which the use of physical force is justified?
- How should parents punish small children?
- How should parents punish teenaged children?
- Should spanking be illegal?

Write a statement of opinion (thesis statement) about the issue.

_____
_____
_____

Write three supporting arguments:

1. _____
   _____

2. _____
   _____

3. _____
   _____

Childhood and Innocence

READING 5.1

Childhood: A Time of Innocence?

by Adele Berridge

1. The conservative film critic, Michael Medved, has written a book called *Saving Childhood*. He is part of a movement of folks who believe that children are exposed to too much sex and violence. His followers indignantly point out that some schools teach young children about masturbation in sex-ed classes. These critics bellow about the violence on television.

2. They worry that children are getting exposed to adult issues at a young age.

3. The "saving childhood" movement thinks the world should revert to a time when children passed thirteen or fourteen years in sweet, simple innocence.

4. The problem is, such a time has never existed.

5. We tend to look at past centuries fondly: we imagine that children were protected from adult concerns. We think that children could frolic in fields without a care, never thinking or worrying about sex, violence, or AIDS.

6. The reality was somewhat different. Children have been robbed of "childhood" throughout history.

7. In past centuries, parents and teachers could physically whip or strap children. Kids did hard work in factories and fields; nobody worried about the exploitation of child laborers. Children were like miniature adults but had fewer rights and privileges.

8. Think about the years of the Irish potato famine. In 1848, orphaned youngsters were sent by the shipload to North America. Upon arrival, the majority of the children were given to families where they became unpaid servants. Sure, they escaped the famine. But no one worried about saving their innocence.

9 Danny, the father of a friend, grew up in the 1930s. By the age of ten, he was herding the neighbour's cattle after school. When he turned twelve, he went to work in the kitchen of a local restaurant. The restaurant owner spent the latter part of the day in a back room smoking opium and he kindly introduced little Danny to the practice.

10 Childhood innocence, eh?

11 This recent insistence on the sacredness of childhood has even reached the justice system.

12 In 1995, a former Mouseketeer, Billie Jean Matay, took her grandkids to Disneyland. She got robbed in the parking lot. Then when the family went to complain to Disney officials in the back office, Matay's grandchildren saw some Disney characters remove their fuzzy heads to reveal the all-too-human face beneath.

13 In true American fashion, Matay sued Disney. She wanted damages not only for being robbed in the Disney parking lot, but also for the "trauma to the children." She argued that her grandchildren were irrevocably hurt when they discovered that Mickey Mouse and Goofy aren't real.

14 Come on! Children will discover what is real and what is fantasy on their own, and there is nothing adults can do to stop it.

15 My own belief in Santa was shattered when I was about six. During a game of frozen tag on our front lawn, a young friend sweetly asked, "Do you believe in Santa?"

16 "Yes, I do," I solemnly replied.

17 "Well, Santa's not real," she announced, triumphantly.

18 I had secretly suspected as much. What kid doesn't look at Santa's beard and wonder why there's a seam under the mouth?

19 And at about the same age, I shattered a neighborhood boy's illusions. Murray came to my back door and offered me some dandelions. His eyes had an adorable, wide-open look as he shyly told me that he loved me.

20 My response? I called him stupid.

21 His little face fell, he dropped the flowers, and he likely decided, from that day forth, to be a little more guarded around women.

22 The bottom line is, you can't stop children from discovering the nasty underbelly of life. I am as sad as the next person when a child's affectionate kiss turns into a surly "I don't care" toss of the head. But children will grow up and get disillusioned. We adults have to accept that fact.

VOCABULARY

1. Find a word in paragraph 1 that means "angrily; resentfully." _____

2. Define **fondly** (paragraph 5). _____

3. Find a verb in paragraph 13 that means "to take legal action against somebody."

4 A *seam* (paragraph 18) is:
 a) a line of stitching   b) food   c) white hair

5 What is the meaning of the expression **from that day forth** (paragraph 21)? Write another phrase that means the same thing.

_____

COMPREHENSION

1 What introduction style is used in this text? Choose one:
 a) anecdote
 b) opposite view
 c) historical background
 d) general background

2 Is this text objective or subjective? _____

If you answered subjective, quote from a paragraph in which the author expresses her opinion or her bias.

_____
_____

3 Why is Michael Medved concerned about children?

_____
_____

4 According to the author, children in the past
 a) had many responsibilities.
 b) were exposed to "bad" things and "bad" people.
 c) were often exploited by employers.
 d) all of the answers

5 What is the main idea of paragraph 9?
 a) Danny, a boy who lived in the 1930s, did not have an innocent childhood.
 b) Danny became an opium addict.
 c) Children need to be protected from a life of labour.
 d) Children were not so innocent in the past.

6 What is the author's main point in paragraphs 14 to 20?

_____

7 What is the author's central thesis? Find one sentence in the text that best sums up the author's main point.

_____
_____

DISCUSSION

1 According to Michael Medved, children are exposed to too much sex and violence. Do you agree? Does exposure to media-related sex and violence harm children?

2 Did you believe in fantasy figures such as Santa Claus when you were a child? Is it harmful or helpful for children to have such beliefs?

Reading Tip:
Think about the Story (plot)

Like essays, short stories generally have a certain structure.

- In the beginning of the story, we are introduced to the characters and the place of the action.
- A problem arises that makes the events more complicated.
- Generally the problem includes some type of conflict (a struggle between opposing forces).
- The conflict generates a series of events that build tension and suspense; it may end in a climactic scene.
- Some events happen to partially resolve the conflict. The central character may go through a transformation.
- The story concludes and the situation stabilizes.

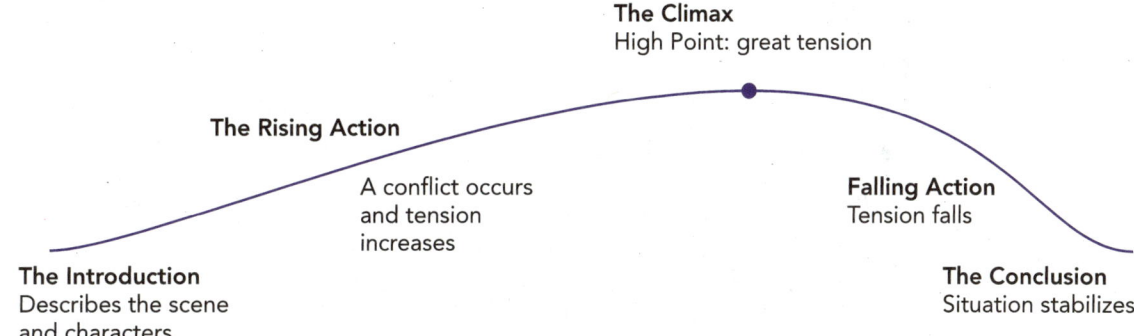

When you summarize the plot of a story, it is important to boil down the story to its basic elements.

READING 5.2

Kurt Vonnegut Jr. is a renowned American author. His novels include *Slaughterhouse Five*, *Mother Night*, and *Breakfast of Champions*. The following short story appeared in his 1968 collection of short stories titled *Welcome to the Monkey House*.

Read the following short story. Afterwards, you will prepare a plot summary.

OPTIONAL ACTIVITIES

Instead of assigning this text as homework, the teacher could present the story in either of the following ways. You will notice that the story is divided into six sections.

1) Retell the Story

- Students are divided into groups. There should be six different groups of roughly equal sizes. Each group is assigned a section of the story.
- Each group reads its section of the story and summarizes it. The summary should include the most important elements of that scene. Each student could summarize his or her section alone, or students could prepare the summary with others who have read the same section.
- Then six students (at least one student for each of the six sections) sit together and retell the story in proper sequence. Together the six students then fill in the plot summary that follows the story.

2) Act It Out

Groups of students could act out each section of the story. Students would read the lines of different characters.

(Note to the teacher: the Instructor's Manual contains a script and more details about how to act out the story.)

Next Door

by Kurt Vonnegut Jr.

Section 1

dwellings
apartments

The old house was divided into two **dwellings** by a thin wall that passed on, with high fidelity, sounds on either side. On the north side were the Leonards. On the south side were the Hargers.

The Leonards – husband, wife and eight-year-old son – had just moved. And, aware of
5 the wall, they kept their voices down as they argued in a friendly way as to whether or not the boy, Paul, was old enough to be left alone for the evening.

"Shhhh!" said Paul's father.

"Was I shouting?" said his mother. "I was talking in a perfectly normal tone."

"If I could hear Harger pulling a cork, he can certainly hear you," said his father.

10 "I didn't say anything I'd be ashamed to have anybody hear," said Mrs. Leonard.

"You called Paul a baby," said Mr. Leonard. "That certainly embarrasses Paul – and it embarrasses me."

"It's just a way of talking," she said.

"It's a way we've got to stop," he said. "And we can stop treating him like a baby, too –
15 *tonight*. We simply shake his hand, walk out, and go to the movie." He turned to Paul. "You're not afraid – are you, boy?"

"I'll be all right," said Paul. He was very tall for his age, and thin, and had a soft, sleepy, radiant sweetness engendered by his mother. "I'm fine."

"Damn right!" said his father, clouting him on the back. "It'll be an adventure."

20 "I'd feel better about this adventure, if we could get a sitter," said his mother.

"If it's going to spoil the picture for you," said the father, "let's take him with us."

Mrs. Leonard was shocked. "Oh – it isn't for children."

"I don't care," said Paul amiably. The why of their not wanting him to see certain movies, certain magazines, certain books, certain television shows was a mystery he respected.

25 "It wouldn't kill him to see it," said father.

"You *know* what it's about," she said.

"What *is* it about?" said Paul innocently.

Mrs. Leonard looked to her husband for help, and got none. "It's about a girl who chooses her friends unwisely," she said.

30 "Oh," said Paul. "That doesn't sound very interesting."

"Are we going, or aren't we, said Mr. Leonard impatiently. "The show starts in ten minutes."

Mrs. Leonard bit her lip. "All right!" she said bravely. "You lock the windows and the back door, and I'll write down the telephone numbers for the police and the fire department and the theater and Dr. Failey." She turned to Paul. "You *can* dial, can't you, 35 dear?"

"He's been dialing for years!" cried Mr. Leonard.

"Sssssh!" said Mrs. Leonard.

"Sorry," Mr. Leonard bowed to the wall. "My apologies."

"Paul dear," said Mrs. Leonard, "what are you going to do while we're gone?"

40 "Oh – look through my microscope, I guess," said Paul.

"You're not going to be looking at germs, are you?" she said.

"Nope – just hair, sugar, pepper, stuff like that," said Paul.

His mother frowned judiciously. "I think that would be all right, don't you?" she said to Mr. Leonard.

45 "Fine!" said Mr. Leonard. "Just as long as the pepper doesn't make him sneeze!"

"I'll be careful," said Paul.

Mr. Leonard winced. "Shhhhh!" he said.

Section 2

Soon after Paul's parents left, the radio in the Harger apartment went on. It was on softly at first – so softly that Paul, looking through his microscope on the living room coffee 50 table, couldn't make out the announcer's words. The music was frail and dissonant – unidentifiable.

Gamely, Paul tried to listen to the music rather than to the man and woman who were fighting.

Paul squinted through the eyepiece of his microscope at the bit of his hair far below, and he turned a knob to bring the hair into focus. It looked like a glistening brown eel, **flecked** here and there with tiny spectra where the light struck the hair just so.

flecked — marked

There – the voices of the man and women were getting louder again, drowning out the radio. Paul twisted the microscope knob nervously, and the objective lens ground into the glass slide on which the hair rested.

The woman was shouting now.

Paul unscrewed the lens, and examined it for damage. Now the man shouted back – shouted something awful, unbelievable.

Paul got a sheet of lens tissue from his bedroom, and dusted at the frosted dot on the lens, where the lens had bitten into the slide. He screwed the lens back in place.

All was quiet again next door – except for the radio.

Paul looked down into the microscope, down into the milky mist of the damaged lens.

Now the fight was beginning again – louder and louder, cruel and crazy.

Trembling, Paul sprinkled grains of salt on a fresh slide, and put it under the microscope.

The woman shouted again, a high, ragged, poisonous shout.

Paul turned the knob too hard, and the fresh slide cracked and fell in triangles to the floor. Paul stood, shaking, wanting to shout, too – to shout in terror and **bewilderment**. It had to stop. Whatever it was, it *had* to stop!

bewilderment — confusion

"If you're going to yell, turn up the radio!" the man cried.

Paul heard the clicking of the woman's heels across the floor. The radio volume **swelled** until the boom of the bass made Paul feel like he was trapped in a drum.

swelled — increased

"And now!" bellowed the radio," for Katy from Fred. For Nancy from Bob, who thinks she's swell! For Arthur, from one who's worshipped him from afar for six weeks! Here's *Stardust*! Remember! If you have a dedication, call Milton nine-three-thousand! Ask for All-Night Sam, the record man!"

The music picked up the house and shook it.

A door slammed next door. Now someone hammered on a door.

Paul looked down into his microscope once more, looked at nothing – while a prickling sensation spread over his skin. He faced the truth: the man and woman would kill each other, if he didn't stop them.

He beat on the wall with his fist. "Mr. Harger! Stop it! he cried. "Mrs. Harger! Stop it!"

"For Ollie from Lavinia!" All-Night Sam cried back at him. "For Ruth from Carl, who'll never forget last Tuesday! For Wilber from Mary, who's lonesome tonight! Here's the Sauter-Finnegan Band asking, *Love, What Are You Doing to My Heart*!

Next door, the **crockery** smashed, filling a split second of radio silence. And then the tidal wave of music drowned everything again.

crockery — plates and bowls

Paul stood by the wall, trembling in his helplessness. "Mr. Harger! Mrs. Harger! Please."

"Remember the number!" said All-Night Sam. "Milton nine-three-thousand!"

Dazed, Paul went to the phone and dialed the number.

Section 3

"WJCD," said the switchboard operator.

95 "Would you kindly connect me with All-Night Sam?" said Paul.

"Hello!" said All Night Sam. He was eating, talking with a full mouth. In the background, Paul could hear the sweet, bleating music, the original of what was **rending** the radio next door.

rending — playing loudly on

"I wonder if I might make a dedication," said Paul.

100 "Dunno why not," said Sam. "Ever belong to any organization listed as subversive by the Attorney General's office?"

Paul thought a moment. "Nossir – I don't think so, sir," he said.

"Shoot," said Sam.

"From Mr. Lemuel K. Harger to Mrs. Harger," said Paul.

105 "What's the message?" said Sam.

"I love you," said Paul. 'Let's make up and start all over again."

The woman's voice was so shrill with passion that it cut through the **din** of the radio, and even Sam heard it.

din — noise

"Kid – are you in trouble?" said Sam. "Your folks fighting?"

110 Paul was afraid that Sam would hang up on him if he found out that Paul wasn't a blood relative of the Hargers. "Yessir," he said.

"And you're trying to pull 'em back together with this dedication?" said Sam.

"Yessir," said Paul.

Sam became very emotional. "O.K., kid," he said hoarsely, "I'll give it everything I've got. 115 Maybe it'll work. I once saved a guy from shooting himself the same way."

"How did you do that?" said Paul, fascinated.

"He called up and said he was gonna blow his brains out," said Sam, "and I played *The Bluebird of Happiness*." He hung up.

Paul dropped the telephone into its cradle. The music stopped, and Paul's hair stood on 120 end. For the first time, the fantastic speed of modern communications was real to him, and he was **appalled**.

appalled — horrified

"Folks!" said Sam. "I guess everybody stops and wonders sometimes what the heck he thinks he's doin' with the life the good Lord gave him! It may seem funny to you folks, because I always keep a cheerful front, no matter how I feel inside, that I wonder 125 sometimes, too! And then, just like some angel was trying to tell me, 'Keep going, Sam, keep going,' something like this comes along."

"Folks!" said Sam, "I've been asked to bring a man and his wife back together again through the miracle of radio! I guess there's no sense in kidding ourselves about marriage!

It isn't any bowl of cherries! There's ups and downs and sometimes folks don't see how they can go on!"

Paul was impressed with the wisdom and authority of Sam. Having the radio turned up high made sense now, for Sam was speaking like the right hand man of God.

When Sam paused for effect, all was still next door. Already the miracle was working.

"Now," said Sam, "a guy in my business has to be half musician, half philosopher, half psychiatrist, and half electrical engineer! And if I've learned one thing from working with all you wonderful people out there, it's this: if folks would swallow their self-respect and pride, there wouldn't be any more divorces!"

There were affectionate cooings from next door. A lump grew in Paul's throat as he thought about the beautiful thing he and Sam were bringing to pass.

Section 4

"Folks!" said Sam, "that's all I'm gonna say about love and marriage. That's all anybody needs to know! And now, for Mrs. Lemuel K. Harger, from Mr. Harger – I love you! Let's make up and start all over again!" Sam choked up. "Here's Eartha Kitt, and *Somebody Bad Stole De Wedding Bell!*"

The radio next door went off.

The world lay still.

A purple emotion flooded Paul's being. Childhood dropped away, and he hung, dizzy, on the **brink** of life, rich, violent, rewarding.

brink edge

There was movement next door – slow, foot-dragging movement.

"So," said the woman.

"Charlotte –" said the man uneasily. "Honey – I swear."

"'I love you,'" she said bitterly. "'Let's make up and start all over again.'"

"Baby," said the man desperately, "it's another Lemuel K. Harger. It's got to be!"

"You want your wife back?" she said. "All right – I won't get in her way. She can have you, Lemuel – you jewel beyond price, you."

"*She* must have called the station," said the man.

Lochinvar an unfaithful young man in a poem by Sir Walter Scott

"She can have you, you philandering, two-timing, two bit **Lochinvar**," she said. "But you won't be in very good condition."

"Charlotte – put down that gun," said the man. "Don't do anything you'll be sorry for."

"That's all behind me, you worm," she said.

There were three shots.

Paul ran out into the hall, and bumped into the woman as she burst from the Harger apartment. She was a big, blond woman, all soft and awry, like an unmade bed.

She and Paul screamed at the same time, and then she grabbed him as he started to run.

"You want candy?" she said wildly. "Bicycle?"

165 "No thank you," said Paul shrilly. "Not at this time."

"You haven't seen or heard a thing!" she said. "You know what happens to squealers?"

"Yes!" cried Paul.

mulch pile She dug into her purse, and brought out a perfumed **mulch** of face tissues, bobby pins and cash. "Here!" she panted. "It's yours! And there's more where that came from, if you 170 keep your mouth shut." She stuffed it into his trousers pocket.

She looked at him fiercely, then fled into the street.

Section 5

Paul ran back into his apartment, jumped into bed, and pulled the covers up over his heard. In the hot, dark cave of the bed, he cried because he and All-Night Sam had helped to kill a man.

175 A policeman came clumping into the house very soon, and he knocked on both apartment doors with his billyclub.

Numb, Paul crept out of the hot, dark cave, and answered the door. Just as he did, the door across the hall opened, and there stood Mr. Harger, haggard but whole.

"Yes, sir?" said Harger. He was a small, balding man, with a hairline mustache. "Can I 180 help you?"

"The neighbors heard some shots," said the policeman.

"Really?" said Harger urbanely. He dampened his mustache with the tip of his little finger. "How bizarre. I heard nothing." He looked at Paul sharply. "Have you been playing with your father's guns again, young man?"

185 "Oh, nossir!" said Paul, horrified.

"Where are your folks?" said the policeman to Paul.

"At the movies," said Paul.

"You're all alone?" said the policeman.

"Yessir," said Paul. "It's an adventure."

190 "I'm sorry I said that about the guns," said Harger. "I certainly would have heard any shots in this house. The walls are thin as paper, and I heard nothing."

Paul looked at him gratefully.

"And you didn't hear any shots, either, kid?" said the policeman.

Before Paul could answer, there was a disturbance out on the street. A big, motherly **wailing crying, shouting** 195 woman was getting out of a taxicab and **wailing** at the top of her lungs. "Lem! Lem, baby."

She barged into the foyer, a suitcase bumping against her leg and tearing her stocking to shreds. She dropped the suitcase, and ran to Harger, throwing her arms around him.

"I got your message, darling," she said, "and I did just what All-Night Sam told me to 200 do. I swallowed my self-respect, and here I am!"

"Rose, Rose, Rose – my little Rose," said Harger. "Don't ever leave me again." They grappled with each other affectionately, and staggered into their apartment.

"Just look at this apartment!" said Mrs. Harger. "Men are just lost without women!" As she closed the door, Paul could see that she was awfully pleased with the mess.

"You *sure* you didn't hear any shots?" said the policeman to Paul.

The ball of money in Paul's pocket seemed to swell to the size of a watermelon. "Yessir," he croaked.

The policeman left.

Paul shut his apartment door, shuffled into his bedroom, and collapsed on the bed.

Section 6

The next voices Paul heard came from his own side of the wall. The voices were sunny – the voices of his mother and father. His mother was singing a nursery rhyme and his father was undressing him.

"Diddle-diddle-dumpling, my son John," piped his mother, "Went to bed with his stockings on. One shoe off, and one shoe on – diddle-diddle-dumpling, my son John."

Paul opened his eyes.

"Hi, big boy," said his father, "you went to sleep with all your clothes on."

"How's my little adventurer?" said his mother.

"O.K.," said Paul sleepily. "How was the show?"

"It wasn't for children, honey," said his mother. "You would have liked the short subject, though. It was all about bears – **cunning** little cubs."

cunning: intelligent

Paul's father handed her Paul's trousers, and she shook them out, and hung them neatly on the back of a chair by the bed. She patted them smooth, and felt the ball of money in the pocket. "Little boy's pockets!" she said, delighted. "Full of childhood's mysteries. An enchanted frog? A magic pocket-knife from a fairy princess?" She caressed the lump.

"He's not a little boy – he's a big boy," said Paul's father. "And he's too old to be thinking about fairy princesses."

Paul's mother held up her hands. "Don't rush it, don't rush it. When I saw him asleep there, I realized all over again how **dreadfully** short childhood is." She reached into the pocket and sighed wistfully. "Little boys are so hard on clothes – especially pockets."

dreadfully: terribly; extremely

She brought out the ball and held it under Paul's nose. "Now, would you mind telling Mommy what we have here?" she said gaily.

The ball bloomed like a frowzy chrysanthemum, with ones, fives, tens, twenties, and lipstick-stained Kleenex for petals. And rising from it, befuddling Paul's young mind, was the pungent must of perfume.

Paul's father sniffed the air. "What's that smell?" he said.

Paul's mother rolled her eyes. "*Tabu*,"[1] she said.

1. *Tabu* is a perfume. It is also a pun: *Taboo* means "something forbidden or unmentionable."

COMPREHENSION

Plot Summary

Fill in the following elements of the story.

- The introduction. Where does the story take place? Describe the opening scene and characters.

  _____
  _____
  _____
  _____

- The rising action. What problem or conflict occurs? What causes the tension to rise?

  _____
  _____
  _____
  _____

- The climax. What is the moment of greatest tension in the story?

  _____
  _____
  _____
  _____

- The falling action. What events tie up loose ends in the story?

  _____
  _____
  _____
  _____

- The ending. How does the story conclude? How has the main character changed?

  _____
  _____
  _____
  _____

Think about the Message

1. Paul's parents go to a movie. What is the movie about? (Try to read between the lines!)
   _____

2. Why don't they want to bring Paul to the movie?
   _____

3. Paul's mother and father disagree about Paul's maturity. What is the mother's point of view?
   _____

   What is the father's point of view?
   _____

4. What three shocking things does Paul learn while his parents are at the movie?
   _____
   _____
   _____

5. Paul's parents don't want to expose him to an "adult" movie. Why is this situation ironic?
   _____
   _____
   _____

6. What is the message of this story?
   _____
   _____

PUNCTUATION

Punctuate the following dialogue. Make sure your quotation marks are in the correct position. Try to do it on your own, and then check how these lines were punctuated in lines 150-152.

1. Charlotte – said the man uneasily. Honey – I swear .

2. I love you, she said bitterly. Let's make up and start all over again.

3. Baby, said the man desperately, it's another Lemuel K. Harger. It's got to be!

Why does the second line have double quotation marks?
_____

LANGUAGE

Recognizing Personification

1 *Personification* is the action of attributing human qualities to inanimate things. For example, *the wind kicked the leaves*. Find two examples of personification in Section 2 of the story.

_____
_____
_____

Recognizing dialogue

Normally, the following terms would not be used in writing. However, writers sometimes incorporate slang and street English into their short story dialogues. What is the correct way to write the following italicized words?

EXAMPLE:

DIALOGUE	LINE NUMBER	CORRECT ENGLISH FORM
2 *Yessir*, said Paul.	113	Yes Sir.
3 *Dunno why not?*	100	
4 You're trying to *pull 'em* back together?	112	
5 … he was *gonna blow* his brains out	117	
6 I guess everybody stops and wonders sometimes *what the heck he thinks he's doin'*	122	
7 … that's all I*'m gonna* say	140	

8 Remember that the incorrect English is used for effect. Notice that Paul's parents do not use slang or incorrect English, but All-Night Sam does. What is the writer probably trying to suggest with such language variations?

_____
_____
_____

Do not use "street English" in your academic writing!

How to Raise a Well-Adjusted Child

With a group of other students, come up with some rules for raising children. You can think about your own experiences when you were a child. Write your guidelines on a sheet of paper. To help you think of some rules, discuss the following questions.

1. How should parents discipline young children?
2. How should parents discipline older children and teenagers?
3. At what age should children be allowed to stay home alone? Why?
4. Should children be allowed to watch films that contain adult subject matter? What *is* adult subject matter?
5. How should parents treat the issue of cigarette smoking?
6. How should parents treat the issues of drinking and drug taking?

Now write down some steps for raising a well-adjusted child.

Essay Topics

Write a text about one of the following subjects. Your text should have an introduction, two or three reasons for your opinion, and a conclusion. (If you did the warm-up activity, you can use the thesis statement and arguments that your team developed.)

Topics:

- Children who swear
- Disciplining children
- Sperm-donor children's rights
- Children need to learn from their own experiences.

More tips about reading fiction.
www.bedfordstmartins.com/litlinks/fiction/readfict.htm

If you want to read some classic short stories, try the following web site.
mbhs.bergtraum.k12.ny.us/cybereng/shorts/

If you want more information about Kurt Vonnegut, try this site:
www.duke.edu/~crh4/vonnegut/

CHAPTER 6 Initiation

Thou know'st the over-eager vehemence of youth. How quick in temper, and in judgement weak.
— Homer

Think about Homer's statement. What does it mean? Is it a fair assessment of youth? In this chapter you will consider youth culture in contemporary and past eras.

Initiation Rituals

Discuss the following questions with a small group of classmates.

1. Certain cultures have specific "coming of age" ceremonies. For example, in the Jewish religion, youths have Bar Mitzvahs; in Mexico, fifteen-year-old females have "quince años" parties to celebrate their blooming adulthood. What other coming of age ceremonies or events do youths have in your culture?

2. What characteristics distinguish adolescence from other stages of life?

3. What are the most important issues facing your generation today?

4. What will your generation be remembered for? Think about youth movements, politics, music, youth fashion, hairstyles, etc.

Youth Culture

Your teacher will divide the class into six teams (one for each time period in the chart). Each team will find some information about a different era and present its findings to the class. If possible, bring in pictures and short audio clips about the era. There are lists of relevant web sites at the end of this chapter.

For each era, find the following information:

- The major youth group's philosophy or reason for rebelling.
- Music, art or literature of that era.
- Hair and fashion styles.
- The major political issues of that era.

You don't have to make a long presentation. Just present information that you find most interesting.

Remember that each generation may have many different youth movements. The ones listed below are among the most memorable of those eras.

THE 1920s	1940s	1950s	1960s	1970s	1990s
The Flappers	The Beat Generation	Greasers, Rockers	Hippies	Punks	Rappers Grunge movement

DISCUSSION

1. Is there any fashion or hairstyle that hasn't been adopted by teenagers? What rebellious "look" could contemporary youths adopt?

2. What are the names of some current youth subcultures?

Alternative Cultures

READING 6.1

In the following article, Veena Thomas dissects "alternative" culture. This article appeared in *The Tech*, MIT University's student newspaper, on November 21, 2000.

VOCABULARY

As you read, you will come across words in bold. In the space provided, write a synonym for that word. Use context clues! The first one has been done for you.

The Real Alternative

by Veena Thomas

1. It's become increasingly hard for a teenager to rebel against the mainstream. Dying hair punk colors has become passé. Goths with white face powder, dark lipstick, and lots of eyeliner no longer attract even a second glance. Everyone listens to "alternative" music. In an era where alternative has become **mainstream**, and becoming mainstream is the only way to rebel, what's an angst-ridden teenager to do?

   conventional

2. The 1960s saw the hippie era, as young adults rebelled by protesting against injustice, the Vietnam War, and the restrictions of society. LSD, marijuana, and free love reigned. Flash forward to the 1970s, when unemployed youths railed against consumer culture and the punk movement began with bands such as the Sex Pistols. Kurt Cobain in the

early 1990s became the **rallying** cry for a new generation of teenagers disillusioned with the confines of society. But what about now?

3 Teenagers **struggling** to be different find themselves with a lack of choices. While "alternative" actually meant something in the early 1990s, now it has become more of an all-encompassing genre meaning, "whatever music teenagers listen to these days." Most of it sounds the same. Perhaps this is why BMG Music Service wisely abandoned the "alternative" music preference category, realizing it has become meaningless. Young adults who once embraced the term "alternative" now frown with disgust and **flock** to punk music or the new heavy metal/rap hybrid.

Sid Vicious and his girlfriend Nancy. Sid was in the 1976 band The Sex Pistols.

4 What should a young punk wear? Previously, rebellious teenagers had to resort to shopping in thrift stores or making their own clothes to attain their desired fashion statement. Luckily (or unluckily) for them, society now makes it easy to dress like an individual. Companies make jeans that already have holes in them so you don't have to wait around to get that punk look. Want to look different? Try Urban Outfitters, the trendy chain store for people fed up with **trendy** chain stores, where you can look "unique" just like everyone else who shops there.

5 With this watering-down of alternative culture, it has become harder and harder to shock anyone or gain any notorious press. Marilyn Manson, the press's former whipping boy and scapegoat for music as a cause of violence in society (witness the aftermath of the Columbine shootings), has faded from the public's view. After **donning** breasts on his videos, concerts, and CD cover to attract attention, Manson realized that breasts were nothing new to half of society and removed them.

6 Now Manson announces that, surprisingly, he'd like George W. Bush to become our next president. Why, you ask? "I think that art, and especially music, thrives under conservative rule," Manson said to MTV's Kurt Loder. "I think that Bill Clinton's attempt to be friends with younger people, to come on MTV – it did something to the rebellion barometer. I don't really support Bush, but I hope we get some good, right-wing, Manson-hating people in office so that I can **piss them off** like I'm supposed to."

7 Indeed, now that Manson has lost his shock value, it takes someone as extreme as Eminem to raise hell in America. Eminem has gathered more than enough press for his songs about killing his wife and other controversial topics. Even his own mother is **suing** him for defamation of character.

8 Eminem has become a strange symbol for the increasingly difficult quest to be different from everyone else, to shock society into paying attention.

9 Perhaps being truly alternative now means thinking for yourself. Be yourself, no matter what that might be. Dress as punk or as preppy as you like. Don't let society's version of "alternative" control your actions. The truly cool can think for themselves.

COMPREHENSION

1 How does Thomas introduce her topic? What introduction style does she use?

_____

2 In paragraph 2, why does Thomas compare contemporary youths to those in the 1960s, 1970s, and 1980s? What is her point?

_____
_____
_____

3 In paragraph 4, Thomas says, "society now makes it easy to dress like an individual." How is this statement ironic?

_____
_____

4 What is not true, according to paragraph 6? Choose the best answer.
   a) Marilyn Manson wants George Bush to be president.
   b) According to Manson, youths felt very rebellious when Bill Clinton was president.
   c) Youth culture (art and music) are more vibrant and rebellious when the government is conservative.
   d) Manson really wants people who hate him to get elected.

5 According to Veena Thomas, what is the central problem for contemporary youths? Write a sentence from the text that best sums up the central problem.

_____
_____

6 What is Thomas's solution to the central problem?

_____
_____

Reading Tip:
Think about the Setting and Characters

In this chapter, you will read a short story. All stories have a basis in a particular time, place, and culture.

SETTING (TIME AND PLACE)

The setting has an important influence on a story. When you read a short story, think about the time and place in which the story occurred. Ask yourself the following questions:

- Where does the story take place? Think about the specific location (house, office, park, etc.) as well as the more general location (suburb, inner city, town, country).
- When does the action occur?
- What was happening in society at that time? Think about major political, cultural and social events.

CHARACTERS

Often the most memorable element of a short story is the characters. Although characters vary tremendously from story to story, they can be categorized into two types: those who evolve and those who remain static. Dynamic characters evolve during the course of a story. They may learn something new or behave in a different manner. Static characters do not evolve and their personalities do not change. When you think about character, ask yourself the following questions:

- What do you know about the main character? What is the main character's background and personality?
- Does the main character evolve? Learn something new? Develop a changed personality?
- Who or what is the main character in conflict with?
- Who are the secondary characters, and how important are they to the story?

Main Events of the 1920s

The 1920s was an exciting period for youths. To help you understand F. Scott Fitzgerald's story, "Bernice Bobs Her Hair," read the following information about this era.

Politics

- **Post World War I Prosperity:** North American economies were booming. This prosperity ended with the stock market crash of 1929. (The 1930s were the years of the Great Depression.)
- **Women's Vote:** Women were given the vote in the United States (1920) and in most Canadian provinces (1922). In 1928, the Supreme Court of Canada refused to allow women to hold public office because women were not defined as "persons." In 1929, the British Privy Council reversed the Supreme Court decision of 1928; women were legally declared "persons" and thus allowed to hold office.
- **Technology:** The car became less expensive and more popular. Young people used the back seat of cars to engage in "petting." Airplanes also became common. Motion picture theaters were in just about every town and city. Silent movies became "talkies" in 1927.

Culture and Society

A new youth movement arose: members called themselves the "flappers."

Louise Brooks was a celebrated silent-film actress. Her "bobbed" hair was her trademark.

- **Flapper fashion:** Young women gave up long heavy dresses and whalebone corsets to dress in knee-length dresses. Since legs were considered highly sexual features of a woman's body, this public exposure of legs was shocking.

- Women no longer padded their bust and rear: instead, flappers tightly wrapped up their breasts to look like boys.

- Flappers wore make-up such as rouge and lipstick. The wearing of make-up was associated with prostitutes and was shocking for parents in the 1920s.

- **Flapper hair:** In the early 1900s, the "Gibson Girl" was popular. She prided herself on her long, beautiful hair that she wore in a loose bun on top of her head. People were shocked when flappers "bobbed" their hair into a short hairstyle.

- **Social Activities:** Black-influenced jazz music was popular. The music and dance styles were considered indecent and wild by older generations.

- For the first time, girls smoked. Even more shocking, they drank alcohol during the Prohibition years. Alcohol could not be legally sold in the United States during the 1920s, but it was easy to find in jazz clubs.

- **Dating:** Before the 1920s, girls could not "date" and a young woman could not be alone with a man unless he was interested in marriage. In the 1920s that changed: the new generation of females didn't want to wait around for men to show interest. "Petting parties" became common. For the first time, a girl could kiss different boys and still have the respect of her social group.

READING 6.2

The next story was written by the American author, F. Scott Fitzgerald (1896-1940). Although he was a hard-drinking, hard-living author, he was able to churn out 160 short stories and four novels, including *The Great Gatsby*. His fiction is very rooted in its time and place but it also contains universal themes. Read the following story, and answer the questions that follow each part of the story.

Bernice Bobs Her Hair

by F. Scott Fitzgerald
(abridged)

Part I

Warren McIntyre, who casually attended Yale, felt in his dinner-coat pocket for a cigarette and strolled out onto the wide, semidark veranda.

Warren was nineteen and rather pitying with those of his friends who hadn't gone East to college. But, like most boys, he bragged tremendously about the girls of his city when he was away from it. There was Genevieve Ormonde, who regularly made the rounds of dances, house-parties, and football games at Princeton, Yale, Williams, and Cornell; and, of course, there was Marjorie Harvey, who besides having a fairylike face and a **dazzling, bewildering tongue** was justly celebrated for having turned five cart-wheels in succession.

Warren, who had grown up across the street from Marjorie, had long been "crazy about her." Sometimes she seemed to reciprocate his feeling with a faint gratitude, but she had tried him by her infallible test and informed him gravely that she did not love him. Her test was that when she was away from him she forgot him and had affairs with other boys. Warren found this discouraging, especially as Marjorie had been making little trips all summer, and for the first two or three days after each arrival home he saw great heaps of mail on the Harveys' hall table addressed to her in various masculine handwritings. To make matters worse, all during the month of August she had been visited by her cousin Bernice from Eau Claire, and it seemed impossible to see her alone.

Much as Warren worshipped Marjorie, he had to admit that Cousin Bernice was **sorta dopeless**. She was pretty, with dark hair and high color, but she was no fun at a party. Every Saturday night he danced a long arduous duty dance with her to please Marjorie, but he had never been anything but bored in her company.

"Warren" – a soft voice at his elbow broke in upon his thoughts, and he turned to see Marjorie, flushed and radiant as usual. "Warren," she whispered, "do something for me – dance with Bernice. She's been stuck with little Otis Ormonde for almost an hour."

"Why – sure," he answered half-heartedly.

"You don't mind, do you? I'll see that you don't get stuck."

"All right."

Marjorie smiled – that smile that was thanks enough.

He wandered back inside, and there in front of the women's dressing-room he found Otis in the centre of a group of young men who were convulsed with laughter. Otis was brandishing a piece of timber he had picked up, and discoursing volubly.

"She's gone in to fix her hair," he announced wildly. "I'm waiting to dance another hour with her. Why don't some of you **cut in**?" cried Otis resentfully. "She likes more variety."

"Why, Otis," suggested a friend, "you've just barely got used to her."

"Why the **two-by-four**, Otis?" inquired Warren, smiling.

"The two-by-four? Oh, this? This is a club. When she comes out I'll hit her on the head and knock her in again."

Warren **collapsed on a settee and howled with glee**. "Never mind, Otis," he articulated finally. "I'm relieving you this time."

No matter how beautiful or brilliant a girl may be, the reputation of not being frequently cut in on makes her position at a dance unfortunate. Youth in this jazz-nourished generation is temperamentally restless, and the idea of fox-trotting more than one full fox trot with the same girl is distasteful, not to say odious. When it comes to several dances and the intermissions between she can be quite sure that a young man, once relieved, will never tread on her wayward toes again.

Warren danced the next full dance with Bernice, and finally, thankful for the intermission, he led her to a table on the veranda. There was a moment's silence while she did unimpressive things with her fan.

50 "It's hotter here than in Eau Claire," she said.

Warren stifled a sigh and nodded. It might be for all he knew or cared. He wondered idly whether she was a poor conversationalist because she got no attention or got no attention because she was a poor conversationalist.

"You going to be here much longer?" he asked.

"Another week," she answered, and stared at him as if to lunge at his next remark when it left his lips.

Warren fidgeted. Then with a sudden charitable impulse he decided to try part of his line on her. He turned and looked at her eyes.

"You've got an awfully kissable mouth," he began quietly.

60 This was a remark that he sometimes made to girls when they were talking in the half dark. Bernice distinctly jumped. She turned an ungraceful red and became clumsy with her fan. No one had ever made such a remark to her before.

"Fresh!" – the word had slipped out before she realized it, and she bit her lip. Too late she decided to be amused, and offered him a **flustered** smile.

Warren was annoyed. Though not accustomed to having that remark taken seriously, still it usually provoked a laugh. And he hated to be called fresh, except in a joking way. His charitable impulse died and he switched the topic.

"Jim Strain and Ethel Demorest sitting out as usual," he commented.

A faint regret mingled with her relief as the subject changed. Men did not talk to her 70 about kissable mouths, but she knew that they talked in some such way to other girls.

"Oh, yes," she said, and laughed. "I hear they've been **mooning round for years without a red penny**. Isn't it silly?"

Warren's disgust increased. Jim Strain was a close friend of his brother's, and anyway he considered it bad form to **sneer** at people for not having money. But Bernice had had no intention of sneering. She was merely nervous.

> **flustered** uncomfortable; nervous
>
> **mooning around for years without a red penny** doing nothing and not earning any money
>
> **sneer** an unkind look or comment that shows you have no respect for someone

Think about the Story

1 Describe the opening scene. Where are the characters? What is happening?

_____

_____

_____

Part II

When Marjorie and Bernice reached home at half after midnight they said good night at the top of the stairs. Though cousins, they were not intimates. As a matter of fact Marjorie had no female intimates – she considered girls stupid. Bernice on the contrary all through this parent-arranged visit had rather longed to exchange confidences. But in this respect she found Marjorie rather cold; felt somehow the same difficulty in talking to her that she had in talking to men. Marjorie never giggled, was never frightened, seldom embarrassed, and in fact had very few of the qualities which Bernice considered appropriately and blessedly feminine.

As Bernice busied herself with tooth-brush and paste this night she wondered for the hundredth time why she never had any attention when she was away from home. That her family were the wealthiest in Eau Claire; that her mother entertained tremendously, gave little dinners for her daughter before all dances and bought her a car of her own to drive round in, never occurred to her as factors in her home-town social success.

Bernice felt a vague pain that she was not at present engaged in being popular. She did not know that had it not been for Marjorie's campaigning she would have danced the entire evening with one man; but she knew that even in Eau Claire other girls with less position were **given a much bigger rush**. She attributed this to something subtly unscrupulous in those girls. It had never worried her, and if it had her mother would have assured her that the other girls cheapened themselves and that men really respected girls like Bernice.

She turned out the light in her bathroom, and on an impulse decided to go in and chat for a moment with her aunt Josephine, whose light was still on. Her soft slippers bore her noiselessly down the carpeted hall, but hearing voices inside she stopped near the partly opened door. Then she caught her own name, and without any definite intention of eavesdropping, she lingered – and the thread of the conversation going on inside pierced her consciousness sharply as if it had been drawn through with a needle.

"She's absolutely hopeless!" It was Marjorie's voice. "Oh, I know what you're going to say! So many people have told you how pretty and sweet she is, and how she can cook! What of it? Men don't like her."

"What's a little cheap popularity?" Mrs. Harvey sounded annoyed.

"It's everything when you're eighteen," said Marjorie emphatically. "I've done my best. I've been polite and I've made men dance with her, but they just won't stand being bored. When I think of that gorgeous coloring wasted on such a **ninny**, and think what Martha Carey could do with it – oh!"

"There's no courtesy these days." Mrs. Harvey's voice implied that modern situations were too much for her. When she was a girl all young ladies who belonged to nice families had glorious times.

"Well," said Marjorie, "no girl can permanently bolster up a **lame-duck** visitor, because these days it's every girl for herself. I've even tried to drop her hints about clothes and things, and she's been furious – given me the funniest looks. I'll bet she consoles herself by thinking that she's very virtuous and that I will come to a bad end. All unpopular girls

---

given a much bigger rush
given more attention

ninny
idiot

lame duck
boring, unpopular

think that way. Sour grapes! Sarah Hopkins refers to Genevieve and Roberta and me as gardenia girls! I'll bet she'd give ten years of her life and her European education to be a gardenia girl and have three or four men in love with her and be cut in on every few feet at dances."

"It seems to me," interrupted Mrs. Harvey rather wearily, "that you ought to be able to do something for Bernice. I know she's not very vivacious."

Marjorie groaned.

"Vivacious! Good grief! I've never heard her say anything to a boy except that it's hot or the floor's crowded or that she's going to school in New York next year. Sometimes she asks them what kind of car they have and tells them the kind she has. Thrilling!"

There was a short silence, and then Mrs. Harvey took up her refrain:

"All I know is that other girls not half so sweet and attractive get partners. Martha Carey, for instance, is stout and loud, and her mother is distinctly common. "

"But, mother," objected Marjorie impatiently, "Martha is cheerful and awfully witty and an awfully **slick** girl."

slick
polished, efficient

Mrs. Harvey yawned.

"I think it's that crazy Indian blood in Bernice," continued Marjorie. "Maybe she's a reversion to type. Indian women all just sat round and never said anything."

"Go to bed, you silly child," laughed Mrs. Harvey. "I wouldn't have told you that if I'd thought you were going to remember it. And I think most of your ideas are perfectly idiotic," she finished sleepily.

There was another silence, while Marjorie considered whether or not convincing her mother was worth the trouble. People over forty can seldom be permanently convinced of anything. At eighteen our convictions are hills from which we look; at forty-five they are caves in which we hide.

Having decided this, Marjorie said good night. When she came out into the hall it was quite empty.

Think about the Story

2 Describe Bernice and Marjorie.

_____
_____
_____

3 How does Marjorie feel about Bernice?

_____
_____

4 How does Bernice feel about Marjorie?

_____

_____

5 What causes the tension to rise?

_____

Part III

While Marjorie was breakfasting late the next day Bernice came into the room with a rather formal good morning, sat down opposite, stared intently over and slightly moistened her lips.

"What's on your mind?" inquired Marjorie, rather puzzled.

Bernice paused before she threw her hand-grenade.

"I heard what you said about me to your mother last night."

150 Marjorie was startled, but she showed only a faintly heightened color and her voice was quite even when she spoke.

"Where were you?"

"In the hall. I didn't mean to listen – at first."

After an involuntary look of contempt Marjorie dropped her eyes and became very interested in balancing a stray corn-flake on her finger.

nuisance
irritation

"I guess I'd better go back to Eau Claire – if I'm such a **nuisance**." Bernice's lower lip was trembling violently and she continued on a wavering note: "I've tried to be nice, and – and I've been first neglected and then insulted. No one ever visited me and got such treatment."

160 Marjorie was silent.

drag on you
a pain; an annoyance

unbecoming
unattractive

"But I'm in the way, I see. I'm a **drag on you**. Your friends don't like me." She paused, and then remembered another one of her grievances. "Of course I was furious last week when you tried to hint to me that that dress was **unbecoming**. Don't you think I know how to dress myself?"

"No," murmured Marjorie less than half-aloud.

"What?"

"I didn't hint anything," said Marjorie succinctly. "I said, as I remember, that it was better to wear a becoming dress three times straight than to alternate it with two frights."

"Do you think that was a very nice thing to say?"

170 "I wasn't trying to be nice." Then after a pause: "When do you want to go?"

Bernice drew in her breath sharply.

"Oh!" It was a little half-cry.

Marjorie looked up in surprise.

"Didn't you say you were going?"

"Yes, but –"

"Oh, you were only **bluffing**!"

They stared at each other across the breakfast-table for a moment. Misty waves were passing before Bernice's eyes, while Marjorie's face wore that rather hard expression that she used when slightly intoxicated undergraduates were **making love** to her.

"So you were bluffing," she repeated as if it were what she might have expected.

Bernice admitted it by bursting into tears. Marjorie's eyes showed boredom.

"You're my cousin," sobbed Bernice. "I'm v-v-visiting you. I was to stay a month, and if I go home my mother will know and she'll wah-wonder –"

Marjorie waited until the shower of broken words collapsed into little sniffles.

"I'll give you my month's allowance," she said coldly, "and you can spend this last week anywhere you want. There's a very nice hotel –"

Bernice's **sobs** rose to a flute note, and rising of a sudden she fled from the room.

An hour later, while Marjorie was in the library absorbed in composing one of those non-committal, marvellously elusive letters that only a young girl can write, Bernice reappeared, very red-eyed and consciously calm. She cast no glance at Marjorie but took a book at random from the shelf and sat down as if to read. Marjorie seemed absorbed in her letter and continued writing. When the clock showed noon Bernice closed her book with a snap.

"I suppose I'd better get my railroad ticket."

This was not the beginning of the speech she had rehearsed up-stairs, but as Marjorie was not getting her cues – wasn't urging her to be reasonable; it's all a mistake – it was the best opening she could muster.

"Just wait till I finish this letter," said Marjorie without looking round. "I want to get it off in the next mail."

After another minute, during which her pen scratched busily, she turned round and relaxed with an air of "at your service." Again Bernice had to speak.

"Do you want me to go home?"

"Well," said Marjorie, considering, "I suppose if you're not having a good time you'd better go. No use being miserable."

"Do you think you've treated me very well?"

"I've done my best. You're rather hard material to work with."

The lids of Bernice's eyes reddened. "I think you're hard and selfish, and you haven't a feminine quality in you."

"Oh, my Lord!" cried Marjorie in desperation. "You little nut! Girls like you are responsible for all the tiresome colorless marriages; all those ghastly inefficiencies that pass as feminine qualities. The womanly woman!" continued Marjorie. "Her whole early life is occupied in **whining** criticisms of girls like me who really do have a good time."

whining complaining in an annoying voice

Bernice's jaw descended as Marjorie's voice rose.

"There's some excuse for an ugly girl whining. If I'd been irretrievably ugly I'd never have forgiven my parents for bringing me into the world. But you're starting life without any handicap." Marjorie's little fist clinched. "If you expect me to weep with you you'll be disappointed. Go or stay, just as you like." And picking up her letters she left the room.

When Marjorie returned late in the afternoon she found Bernice with a strangely set face waiting for her in her bedroom.

"I've decided," began Bernice without preliminaries, "that maybe you're right about things – possibly not. But if you'll tell me why your friends aren't – aren't interested in me I'll see if I can do what you want me to."

Marjorie was at the mirror shaking down her hair.

"Do you mean it?"

"Yes."

"Without reservations? Will you do exactly what I say?"

"Well, I –"

"Well nothing! Will you do exactly as I say?"

"If they're sensible things."

"They're not! You're no case for sensible things."

" Are you going to make – to recommend –"

"Yes, everything. If I tell you to take boxing-lessons you'll have to do it. Write home and tell your mother you're going to stay another two weeks."

"If you'll tell me –"

"All right – I'll just give you a few examples now. First, you have no ease of manner. Why? Because you're never sure about your personal appearance. When a girl feels that she's perfectly groomed and dressed she can forget that part of her. That's charm. The more parts of yourself you can afford to forget the more charm you have."

"Don't I look all right?"

"No; for instance, you never take care of your eyebrows. They're black and lustrous, but by leaving them straggly they're a blemish. They'd be beautiful if you'd take care of them in one-tenth the time you take doing nothing. You're going to brush them so that they'll grow straight."

Bernice raised the brows in question.

"Do you mean to say that men notice eyebrows?"

"Yes – subconsciously. And when you go home you ought to have your teeth straightened a little. It's almost imperceptible, still –"

"But I thought," interrupted Bernice in bewilderment, "that you despised little dainty feminine things like that."

"I hate dainty minds," answered Marjorie. "But a girl has to be dainty in person. If she looks like a million dollars she can talk about Russia, ping-pong, or the League of Nations and get away with it."

"What else?"

"Oh, I'm just beginning! There's your dancing."

"Don't I dance all right?"

"No, you don't – you lean on a man; yes, you do – ever so slightly. I noticed it when we were dancing together yesterday. And you dance standing up straight instead of bending over a little. Probably some old lady on the side-line once told you that you looked so dignified that way. But except with a very small girl it's much harder on the man, and he's the one that counts."

"Go on." Bernice's brain was reeling.

"Well, you've got to learn to be nice to men who are **sad birds**. You look as if you'd been insulted whenever you're thrown with any except the most popular boys. Why, Bernice, I'm cut in on every few feet – and who does most of it? Why, those very sad birds. No girl can afford to neglect them. They're the big part of any crowd. Young boys too shy to talk are the very best conversational practice. Clumsy boys are the best dancing practice. If you can follow them and yet look graceful you can follow a baby tank across a barb-wire sky-scraper."

Bernice sighed profoundly, but Marjorie was not through.

"If you go to a dance and really amuse, say, three sad birds that dance with you; if you talk so well to them that they forget they're stuck with you, you've done something. They'll come back next time, and gradually so many sad birds will dance with you that the attractive boys will see there's no danger of being stuck – then they'll dance with you."

"Yes," agreed Bernice faintly. "I think I begin to see."

"And finally," concluded Marjorie, "poise and charm will just come. You'll wake up some morning knowing you've attained it, and men will know it too."

Bernice rose.

"It's been awfully kind of you – but nobody's ever talked to me like this before, and I feel sort of startled."

Marjorie made no answer but gazed pensively at her own image in the mirror.

"You're a peach to help me," continued Bernice.

Still Marjorie did not answer, and Bernice thought she had seemed too grateful.

"I know you don't like sentiment," she said timidly.

---

sad birds in the context it means "unpopular boys"

Marjorie turned to her quickly.

"Oh, I wasn't thinking about that. I was considering whether we hadn't better bob your hair."

Bernice collapsed backward upon the bed.

> **Think about the Story**
>
> **6** What conflict occurs? How do the girls resolve the tension?
>
> _____
>
> _____
>
> _____

Part IV

On the following Wednesday evening there was a dinner-dance at the country club. When the guests strolled in Bernice found her place-card with a slight feeling of irritation. Though at her right sat G. Reece Stoddard, a most desirable and distinguished young bachelor, the all-important left held only Charley Paulson. Charley lacked height, beauty, and social shrewdness, and in her new enlightenment Bernice decided that his only qualification to be her partner was that he had never been stuck with her. But this feeling of irritation left with the last of the soup-plates, and Marjorie's specific instruction came to her. Swallowing her pride she turned to Charley Paulson and plunged.

"Do you think I ought to bob my hair, Mr. Charley Paulson?"

Charley looked up in surprise.

"Why?"

"Because I'm considering it. It's such a sure and easy way of attracting attention."

Charley smiled pleasantly. He could not know this had been rehearsed. He replied that he didn't know much about bobbed hair. But Bernice was there to tell him.

"I want to be a society vampire, you see," she announced coolly, and went on to inform him that bobbed hair was the necessary prelude. She added that she wanted to ask his advice, because she had heard he was so critical about girls.

Charley, who knew as much about the psychology of women as he did of the mental states of Buddhist contemplatives, felt vaguely flattered.

"So I've decided," she continued, her voice rising slightly, "that early next week I'm going down to the Sevier Hotel barber-shop, sit in the first chair, and get my hair bobbed." She faltered, noticing that the people near her had paused in their conversation and were listening; but after a confused second Marjorie's coaching told, and she finished her paragraph to the vicinity at large. "Of course I'm charging admission, but if you'll all come down and encourage me I'll issue passes for the inside seats."

There was a ripple of appreciative laughter, and under cover of it G. Reece Stoddard leaned over quickly and said close to her ear: "I'll take a box right now."

She met his eyes and smiled as if he had said something surpassingly brilliant.

"Do you believe in bobbed hair?" asked G. Reece in the same undertone.

"I think it's unmoral," affirmed Bernice gravely. "But, of course, you've either got to amuse people or feed 'em or shock 'em." Marjorie had culled this from **Oscar Wilde**. It was greeted with a ripple of laughter from the men and a series of quick, intent looks from the girls. And then as though she had said nothing of wit or moment Bernice turned again to Charley and spoke confidentially in his ear.

"I want to ask you your opinion of several people. I imagine you're a wonderful judge of character."

Charley paid her a subtle compliment by overturning her water.

Two hours later, while Warren McIntyre was standing passively in the **stag line** abstractedly watching the dancers and wondering whither and with whom Marjorie had disappeared, an unrelated perception began to creep slowly upon him – a perception that Bernice, cousin to Marjorie, had been cut in on several times in the past five minutes. He closed his eyes, opened them and looked again. Several minutes back she had been dancing with a visiting boy, a matter easily accounted for; a visiting boy would know no better. But now she was dancing with some one else, and there was Charley Paulson headed for her with enthusiastic determination in his eye. Funny – Charley seldom danced with more than three girls an evening.

Warren was distinctly surprised when – the exchange having been effected – the man relieved proved to be none other than G. Reece Stoddard himself. And G. Reece seemed not at all jubilant at being relieved. Next time Bernice danced near, Warren regarded her intently. Yes, she was pretty, distinctly pretty; and to-night her face seemed really vivacious. She had that look that no woman, however histrionically proficient, can successfully counterfeit – she looked as if she were having a good time. He liked the way she had her hair arranged, wondered if it was brilliantine that made it glisten so. And that dress was becoming – a dark red that set off her shadowy eyes and high coloring. He remembered that he had thought her pretty when she first came to town, before he had realized that she was dull.

His thoughts zigzagged back to Marjorie. This disappearance would be like other disappearances. When she reappeared he would demand where she had been – would be told emphatically that it was none of his business. What a pity she was so sure of him! She **basked** in the knowledge that no other girl in town interested him; she defied him to fall in love with Genevieve or Roberta.

Warren sighed. The way to Marjorie's affections was a labyrinth indeed. He looked up. Bernice was again dancing with the visiting boy. Half unconsciously he took a step out from the stag line in her direction, and hesitated. Then he said to himself that it was charity. He walked toward her and collided suddenly with G. Reece Stoddard.

"Pardon me," said Warren.

But G. Reece had not stopped to apologize. He had again cut in on Bernice.

That night at one o'clock Marjorie, with one hand on the electric-light switch in the hall, turned to take a last look at Bernice's sparkling eyes.

"So it worked?"

"Oh, Marjorie, yes!" cried Bernice.

"I saw you were having a **gay** time."

gay 1920s meaning: "happy; pleasant; fabulous"

360 "I did! The only trouble was that about midnight I ran short of talk. I had to repeat myself – with different men of course. I hope they won't compare notes."

"Men don't," said Marjorie, yawning, "and it wouldn't matter if they did – they'd think you were even trickier."

She snapped out the light, and as they started up the stairs Bernice grasped the banister thankfully. For the first time in her life she had been danced tired.

"You see," said Marjorie at the top of the stairs, "one man sees another man cut in and he thinks there must be something there. Well, we'll fix up some new stuff tomorrow. Good night."

"Good night."

370 As Bernice took down her hair she passed the evening before her in review. She had followed instructions exactly. Even when Charley Paulson cut in for the eighth time she had simulated delight and had apparently been both interested and flattered. She had not talked about the weather or Eau Claire or automobiles or her school, but had confined her conversation to me, you, and us.

But a few minutes before she fell asleep a rebellious thought was churning drowsily in her brain – after all, it was she who had done it. Bernice had bought the red dress, though she had never valued it highly before Marjorie dug it out of her trunk – and her own voice had said the words, her own lips had smiled, her own feet had danced. Marjorie nice girl – vain, though – nice evening – nice boys – like Warren – Warren – Warren –
380 what's-his-name – Warren…

She fell asleep.

> **Think about the Story**
>
> **7** How does Bernice change?
>
> _____
>
> _____
>
> **8** How does Marjorie generally treat Warren?
>
> _____
>
> _____

Part V

To Bernice the next week was a revelation. With the feeling that people really enjoyed looking at her and listening to her came the foundation of self-confidence. Of course there were numerous mistakes at first. She did not know, for instance, that Draycott Deyo was studying for the ministry; she was unaware that he had cut in on her because he thought she was a quiet, reserved girl. Had she known these things she would not have treated him to the line which began "Hello, Shell Shock!" and continued with the bathtub story –"It takes a **frightful** lot of energy to fix my hair in the summer – there's so much of it – so I always fix it first and powder my face and put on my hat; then I get into the bathtub, and dress afterward. Don't you think that's the best plan?"

Though Draycott Deyo was in the throes of difficulties concerning baptism by immersion and might possibly have seen a connection, it must be admitted that he did not. He considered feminine bathing an immoral subject, and gave her some of his ideas on the depravity of modern society.

But to offset that unfortunate occurrence Bernice had several signal successes to her credit. Little Otis Ormonde pleaded off from a trip East and elected instead to follow her with a puppy-like devotion, to the amusement of his crowd. He even told her the story of the two-by-four and the dressing-room to show her how frightfully mistaken he and every one else had been in their first judgment of her. Bernice laughed off that incident with a slight sinking sensation.

Of all Bernice's conversation perhaps the best known and most universally approved was the line about the bobbing of her hair.

"Oh, Bernice, when you goin' to get the hair bobbed?"

"Day after to-morrow maybe," she would reply, laughing. "Will you come and see me? Because I'm counting on you, you know."

But perhaps the most significant symbol of her success was the gray car of the hypercritical Warren McIntyre, parked daily in front of the Harvey house. At first the parlor-maid was distinctly startled when he asked for Bernice instead of Marjorie; after a week of it she told the cook that Miss Bernice had gotta hold a Miss Marjorie's best fella.

And Miss Bernice had. Perhaps it began with Warren's desire to rouse jealousy in Marjorie; perhaps it was the familiar though unrecognized strain of Marjorie in Bernice's conversation; perhaps it was both of these and something of sincere attraction besides. But somehow the collective mind of the younger set knew within a week that Marjorie's most reliable beau had made an amazing about-face and was giving an indisputable rush to Marjorie's guest. The question of the moment was how Marjorie would take it. Warren called Bernice on the 'phone twice a day, sent her notes, and they were frequently seen together in his **roadster**, obviously engrossed in one of those tense, significant conversations as to whether or not he was sincere.

Marjorie only laughed. She said she was mighty glad that Warren had at last found some one who appreciated him. So the younger set laughed, too, and guessed that Marjorie didn't care and let it go at that.

One afternoon when there were only three days left of her visit Bernice was waiting in the hall for Warren, with whom she was going to a bridge party. She was in rather a **blissful** mood, and when Marjorie – also bound for the party – appeared beside her and began casually to adjust her hat in the mirror. Bernice was utterly unprepared for anything in the nature of a clash. Marjorie did her work very coldly and succinctly in three sentences.

> blissful
> extremely happy and serene

"You may as well get Warren out of your head," she said coldly.

"What?" Bernice was utterly astounded.

430 "You may as well stop making a fool of yourself over Warren McIntyre. He doesn't care a snap of his fingers about you."

For a tense moment they regarded each other – Marjorie scornful, aloof; Bernice astounded, half-angry, half-afraid. Then two cars drove up in front of the house and there was a riotous honking. Both of them gasped faintly, turned, and side by side hurried out.

All through the bridge party Bernice strove in vain to master a rising uneasiness. She had offended Marjorie. With the most wholesome and innocent intentions in the world she had stolen Marjorie's property. She felt suddenly and horribly guilty. After the bridge game, when they sat in an informal circle and the conversation became general, the storm gradually broke. Little Otis Ormonde inadvertently precipitated it.

440 "When are you going back to kindergarten, Otis?" someone had asked.

"Me? The day Bernice gets her hair bobbed."

"Then your education's over," said Marjorie quickly. "That's only a bluff of hers. I should think you'd have realized."

"That a fact?" demanded Otis, giving Bernice a reproachful glance.

Bernice's ears burned as she tried to think up an effectual come-back. In the face of this direct attack her imagination was paralyzed.

"There's a lot of bluffs in the world," continued Marjorie quite pleasantly. "I should think you'd be young enough to know that, Otis."

"Well," said Otis, "maybe so. But gee! With **a line** like Bernice's –"

> a line
> a clever, shocking announcement

450 "Really?" yawned Marjorie. "What's her latest bon mot?"

No one seemed to know. In fact, Bernice had said nothing memorable of late.

"Was that really all a line?" asked Roberta curiously.

Bernice hesitated. Under her cousin's suddenly frigid eyes she was completely incapacitated.

"I don't know," she stalled.

"Splush!" said Marjorie. "Admit it!"

Bernice saw that Warren's eyes were fixed on her questioningly. "Oh, I don't know!" she repeated steadily. Her cheeks were glowing.

"Splush!" remarked Marjorie again.

"Come through, Bernice," urged Otis. "Tell her where to get off."

Bernice looked round again – she seemed unable to get away from Warren's eyes. "I like bobbed hair," she said hurriedly, as if he had asked her a question, "and I intend to bob mine."

"When?" demanded Marjorie.

"Any time."

"No time like the present," suggested Roberta.

Otis jumped to his feet.

"Good stuff!" he cried. "We'll have a summer bobbing party. Sevier Hotel barber-shop, I think you said."

In an instant all were on their feet. Bernice's heart throbbed violently.

"What?" she gasped.

Out of the group came Marjorie's voice, very clear and contemptuous. "Don't worry – she'll back out!"

"Come on, Bernice!" cried Otis, starting toward the door.

Four eyes – Warren's and Marjorie's – stared at her, challenged her, defied her. For another second she wavered wildly.

"All right," she said swiftly, "I don't care if I do."

An eternity of minutes later, riding down-town through the late afternoon beside Warren, the others following in Roberta's car close behind, Bernice had all the sensations of Marie Antoinette bound for the guillotine in a tumbrel. Vaguely she wondered why she did not cry out that it was all a mistake. It was all she could do to keep from clutching her hair with both hands to protect it from the suddenly hostile world. Yet she did neither. Even the thought of her mother was no deterrent now. This was the test supreme of her sportsmanship; her right to walk unchallenged in the starry heaven of popular girls.

Warren was moodily silent, and when they came to the hotel he drew up at the curb and nodded to Bernice to precede him out. Roberta's car emptied a laughing crowd into the shop.

Bernice stood on the curb and looked at the sign, Sevier Barber-Shop.

"All right, Bernice," said Warren quickly.

With her chin in the air she crossed the sidewalk, pushed open the swinging screen-door, and went up to the first barber.

"I want you to bob my hair."

The first barber's mouth slid somewhat open. His cigarette dropped to the floor.

"Huh?"

"My hair – bob it!"

Refusing further preliminaries, Bernice took her seat on high. A man in the chair next to her turned on his side and gave her a glance, half lather, half amazement. One barber started and spoiled little Willy Schuneman's monthly haircut.

500 Bernice saw nothing, heard nothing. Her only living sense told her that this man in the white coat had removed one tortoise-shell comb and then another; that his fingers were fumbling clumsily with unfamiliar hairpins; that this hair, this wonderful hair of hers, was going – she would never again feel its long voluptuous pull as it hung in a dark-brown glory down her back. For a second she was near breaking down, and then the picture before her swam mechanically into her vision – Marjorie's mouth curling in a faint ironic smile as if to say: "Give up and get down! You tried to buck me and I called your bluff. "

And some last energy rose up in Bernice, for she clinched her hands under the white cloth, and there was a curious narrowing of her eyes that Marjorie remarked on to some 510 one long afterward.

Twenty minutes later the barber swung her round to face the mirror, and she flinched at the full extent of the damage that had been wrought. Her hair was not curly, and now it lay in lank lifeless blocks on both sides of her suddenly pale face. It was ugly as sin – she had known it would be ugly as sin. Her face's chief charm had been a Madonna-like simplicity. Now that was gone and she was – well, frightfully mediocre – not stagy; only ridiculous, like a Greenwich Villager who had left her spectacles at home.

As she climbed down from the chair she tried to smile-failed miserably. She saw two of the girls exchange glances; noticed Marjorie's mouth curved in **attenuated mockery** – and that Warren's eyes were suddenly very cold.

attenuated mockery ridicule, contempt

520 "You see" – her words fell into an awkward pause – "I've done it."

"Yes, you've – done it," admitted Warren.

"Do you like it?"

There was a half-hearted "Sure" from two or three voices, another awkward pause, and then Marjorie turned swiftly and with serpentlike intensity to Warren. "Would you mind running me down to the cleaners?" she asked. "I've simply got to get a dress there before supper. Roberta's driving right home and she can take the others."

Warren stared abstractedly at some infinite speck out the window. Then for an instant his eyes rested coldly on Bernice before they turned to Marjorie.

"Be glad to," he said slowly.

Think about the Story

9 How does the tension escalate in this scene?

> **10** What incident is the high point (when the action reaches a peak)?
> _____
> _____
>
> **11** How do Marjorie and Warren feel after Bernice cuts her hair?
> _____
> _____

Part VI

530 Bernice did not fully realize the outrageous trap that had been set for her until she met her aunt's amazed glance just before dinner.

"Why, Bernice!"

"I've bobbed it, Aunt Josephine."

"Why, child!"

"I suppose I've shocked you."

"No, but what'll Mrs. Deyo think tomorrow night? Bernice, you should have waited until after the Deyos' dance – you should have waited if you wanted to do that."

"It was sudden, Aunt Josephine. Anyway, why does it matter to Mrs. Deyo particularly?"

foibles
faults; shortcomings; bad habits

540 "Why, child," cried Mrs. Harvey, "in her paper on 'The **Foibles** of the Younger Generation' that she read at the last meeting of the Thursday Club she devoted fifteen minutes to bobbed hair. It's her pet abomination. And the dance is for you and Marjorie!"

"I'm sorry."

"Oh, Bernice, what'll your mother say? She'll think I let you do it."

"I'm sorry."

Dinner was an agony. She had made a hasty attempt with a curling-iron, and burned her finger and much hair. She could see that her aunt was both worried and grieved, and her uncle kept saying, "Well, I'll be darned!" over and over in a hurt and faintly hostile tone. And Marjorie sat very quietly, entrenched behind a faintly mocking smile.

550 Somehow she got through the evening. Three boys called; Marjorie disappeared with one of them, and Bernice made a listless unsuccessful attempt to entertain the two others – sighed thankfully as she climbed the stairs to her room at half past ten. What a day!

When she had undressed for the night the door opened and Marjorie came in.

"Bernice," she said, "I'm awfully sorry about the Deyo dance. I'll give you my word of honor I'd forgotten all about it."

"'It's all right," said Bernice shortly. Standing before the mirror she passed her comb slowly through her short hair.

"I'll take you down-town to-morrow," continued Marjorie, "and the hairdresser'll fix it so you'll look slick. I didn't imagine you'd go through with it. I'm really mighty sorry."

560 "Oh, 'sall right!"

"Still it's your last night, so I suppose it won't matter much."

Then Bernice winced as Marjorie tossed her own hair over her shoulders and began to twist it slowly into two long blond braids until in her cream-colored negligée she looked like a delicate painting of some Saxon princess.

Perhaps by tomorrow Mrs. Deyo would have heard the news; would send round an icy little note requesting that she fail to appear – and behind her back they would all laugh and know that Marjorie had made a fool of her; that her chance at beauty had been sacrificed to the jealous whim of a selfish girl. She sat down suddenly before the mirror, biting the inside of her cheek.

570 "I like it," she said with an effort. "I think it'll be becoming."

Marjorie smiled.

"It looks all right. For heaven's sake, don't let it worry you!"

"I won't."

"Good night, Bernice."

sprang jumped

But as the door closed something snapped within Bernice. She **sprang** dynamically to her feet, clinching her hands, then swiftly and noiselessly crossed over to her bed and from underneath it dragged out her suitcase. Into it she tossed toilet articles and a change of clothing. Then she turned to her trunk and quickly dumped in two drawerfuls of lingerie and summer dresses. She moved quietly, but with deadly efficiency, and in three-
580 quarters of an hour her trunk was locked and strapped and she was fully dressed in a becoming new travelling suit that Marjorie had helped her pick out.

Sitting down at her desk she wrote a short note to Mrs. Harvey, in which she briefly outlined her reasons for going. She sealed it, addressed it, and laid it on her pillow. She glanced at her watch. The train left at one, and she knew that if she walked down to the Marborough Hotel two blocks away she could easily get a taxicab.

Suddenly she drew in her breath sharply and an expression flashed into her eyes that a practised character reader might have connected vaguely with the set look she had worn in the barber's chair – somehow a development of it. It was quite a new look for Bernice and it carried consequences.

590 She went stealthily to the bureau, picked up an article that lay there, and turning out all the lights stood quietly until her eyes became accustomed to the darkness. Softly she pushed open the door to Marjorie's room. She heard the quiet, even breathing of an untroubled conscience asleep.

She was by the bedside now, very deliberate and calm. She acted swiftly. Bending over she found one of the braids of Marjorie's hair, followed it up with her hand to the point nearest the head, and then holding it a little slack so that the sleeper would feel no pull, she

shears scissors

reached down with the **shears** and severed it. With the pigtail in her hand she held her

<small>deftly
skillfully</small>

breath. Marjorie had muttered something in her sleep. Bernice **deftly** amputated the other braid, paused for an instant, and then flitted swiftly and silently back to her own room.

600 Down-stairs she opened the big front door, closed it carefully behind her, and feeling oddly happy and exuberant stepped off the porch into the moonlight, swinging her heavy grip like a shopping-bag. After a minute's brisk walk she discovered that her left hand still held the two blond braids. She laughed unexpectedly – had to shut her mouth hard to keep from emitting an absolute peal. She was passing Warren's house now, and on the impulse she set down her baggage, and swinging the braids like pieces of rope flung them at the wooden porch, where they landed with a slight thud. She laughed again, no longer restraining herself.

"Huh!" she giggled wildly. "Scalp the selfish thing!"

Then picking up her suitcase she set off at a half-run down the moonlit street.

<small>Abridged version of "Bernice Bobs Her Hair," from *Flappers and Philosophers*. New York: Scribners, 1922.</small>

Think about the Story

12 How does the story conclude?

_____

_____

COMPREHENSION

Think about the Time and Place

1 Describe the setting of the story. When and where does most of the action take place?

_____

_____

2 What social class do the main characters belong to? Give some examples from the text to prove your answer.

_____

_____

_____

_____

3 What makes this a "1920s" story? Find a quotation from the text that will illustrate the following elements. Then explain how things are different today.

<u>FOR EXAMPLE:</u> **Fashion**

1920s: *"Bernice had a dark red dress that Warren thought was becoming."*

Today: *Most girls today don't wear dresses.*

a) Hair styles _____
_____

Today: _____

b) Dance etiquette _____
_____

Today: _____

c) Social activities _____
_____

Today: _____

Think about Characterization

4 Describe Bernice's personality at the beginning of the story. Find a quotation to explain what type of person she was.

_____
_____
_____
_____
_____

5 How does Bernice change in the middle of the story? Find a quotation to explain the change that took place.

_____
_____
_____
_____
_____

6 Describe Warren. What type of person is he? Does he change? Explain your answer and find a supporting quotation.

_____
_____
_____
_____

7 Describe Marjorie. What type of person is she? Does she change? Explain your answer and find a supporting quotation.

_____

Think about the Message

8 What is the story's universal message?

_____

DISCUSSION

1 How would you summarize this story? What are the main events?

2 In Part 2 of the text, Marjorie and her mother discuss Bernice's "crazy Indian blood." How do the stereotyped references to "Indians" help situate this story in the 1920s?

Scott and Zelda

F. Scott Fitzgerald was born on September 24, 1896. At age 21, he met and fell in love with a southern girl named Zelda. His first novel, *This Side of Paradise*, was published in 1920 and was extremely successful. In between writing novels, Fitzgerald wrote articles for *The Saturday Evening Post* and became the unofficial spokesman for the young, free-thinking, independent "flapper" generation.

In their early twenties, Scott and Zelda seemingly had it all: love, wealth, and, for Scott, artistic success. But their extravagant living took a toll. By the 1930s, Scott was a hopeless alcoholic and Zelda had a mental breakdown.

You will hear an interview with Canadian Playwright Sharon Pollock. She discusses Scott and Zelda's relationship.

Scott and Zelda on a trip with their daughter.

COMPREHENSION

Answer the following questions.

1 According to Pollock, what kind of person was Scott?

_____

_____

2 What kind of person was Zelda?

_____
_____

3 What type of relationship did Scott and Zelda have?

_____
_____
_____

4 What impact did Zelda have on Scott's writing?

_____
_____
_____

5 In your opinion, why did Scott ask Zelda never to write novels?

_____
_____
_____
_____

6 How does Pollock appear to be biased in her assessment of Scott and Zelda?

_____

What factors could influence her point of view?

_____
_____

DISCUSSION

1 Does the information you have just heard affect your appreciation of the short story, "Bernice Bobs Her Hair," or of Scott's talents as an author?

2 Should judgements about works of art also be based on the artist's personal life? Does it matter if an artist is not a nice person?

Writing Tip: Writing about Fiction

WRITING ABOUT FICTION: WHAT TENSE SHOULD I USE?

- When writing about a fictional short story, generally use the present tense to describe the characters and their situations.

    *Bernice **feels** shy and awkward around boys. She **receives** some advice from her cousin, Marjorie.*

- When writing about historical events, use the past tense.

*In the 1920s, young people **socialized** at dinner parties and in dance clubs.*

WRITING TIP EXERCISE

Identify and correct any incorrect tense usage in the following paragraphs. Note: in past-tense sentences, replace *can* with *could*, and replace *will* with *would*. There are eight tense errors.

1. In the nineteenth century, men and women lived in different spheres. They could meet in public places, but young men and women can never go on dates unless a chaperone was present. Women are considered morally superior to men at that time, but when a man seduced a woman, she will receive the blame. By the 1920s, unchaperoned dating became common and acceptable, and young people openly flirted with the opposite sex.

2. In 1920s jazz clubs, youths meet each other and dance. A girl was popular if many boys "cut in" on her dances. In "Bernice Bobs Her Hair," Bernice is initially unpopular. Boys didn't want to dance with her. Then she learns to entertain her dance partners with sparkling conversation and they started to feel comfortable around her. Bernice becomes popular, but when she decided to cut her hair, her friends desert her.

Essay Topics

Write an essay on one of the following topics. You must include some supporting quotes in your essay.

1. Contemporary youths have (or do not have) a distinguishing culture. You can refer to Veena Thomas's text and decide if you agree or disagree with Thomas.

2. Compare the 1920s to modern times. How are adolescents similar? How are they different?

3. How do the flappers compare to other generations of young people (beats, hippies, punks, rappers, etc.)? Write a text comparing the flappers to other youth movements.

4. The 1920s actress, Tallulah Bankhead, once said, "If I had my life to live over again, I'd make the same mistakes, only sooner." Discuss the importance of making mistakes in the learning process.

Your essay should have an interesting introduction, two or three body paragraphs, and a conclusion.

Do you want to hear some music from the jazz age? Go to the following site and scroll to the bottom of the page. If you have "real audio" you can hear some 1920s jazz. www.bassocantante.com/flapper/music.html or go to vintage recordings at: vintage-recordings.com

The following sites contain information about different decades.

Basic facts about each decade: cdcga.org/HTMLs/decades/1920s.htm (Scroll to the bottom of the page to find the decade that interests you.)

Fashion Through the Decades: www.vintagevixen.com/history/1940s.asp

- **The 1920s**
  The 1920s: www.louisville.edu/~kprayb01/1920s.html
  Flapper culture and style: www.geocities.com/flapper_culture/
  Jazz Age slang: home.earthlink.net/~dlarkins/slang-pg.htm

- **The 1940s**
  The Beat Generation: www.jackmagazine.com/beatnews/
  The Beat writers: www.bohemiabooks.com.au/eblinks/spirboho/modern/beat/beat.htm
  1940s hairstyles: www.retroactive.com/apr99/40shair.html
  Heroes of the 1940s: www.heroism.org/class/1940/

- **The 1950s**
  The "Teddy Boys": www.geocities.com/Nashville/7957/historique.htm
  The 1950s: www.joesherlock.com/fifties.html
  1950s music: www.information-entertainment.com/50com.html
  Elvis Presley: www.elvis.com/

- **The 1960s**
  1960s photos: www2.cea.edu/robert/Page7.MrSixties.html
  The antiwar movement and Woodstock: library.thinkquest.org/27942/counter.htm
  1960s fashion: www.sixtiespop.freeserve.co.uk/fash1.htm
  Music: http://www.rockument.com/haimg.html OR
  oldies.about.com/library/weekly/aa062799.htm?once=true&

- **The 1970s**
  Events of the 1970s: www.idiotsguides.com/QuickGuides/MG_Seventies/file.htm
  The Sex Pistols: www.sex-pistols.net/main.html OR
  www.furious.com/perfect/pistols.html
  Punk roots in America: www.inch.com/~jessamin/intro.html
  Origins of hip-hop: www.harcourtcanada.com/newsociety3e/article.htm

CHAPTER 7 Love

I can resist everything except temptation.
– Oscar Wilde (1856-1900)

Marriage is a great institution, but I'm not ready for an institution.
– Mae West

Is long-lasting monogamous love possible? And what are some myths about love? This chapter focuses on the qualities of love.

Relationship Survey

Take the following relationship quiz.

Attitudes

1 When you fall in love, would you
  a) enjoy it and then move on. Love never lasts.
  b) live common-law and not get married.
  c) get married. It's important to legalize a committed relationship.

2 Does a good marriage always remain romantic? ❑ No ❑ Yes

3 Will a long-term, committed relationship make you happy? ❑ No ❑ Yes

4 Does love just exist or do you have to work at it? ❑ Exists ❑ Work at it

5 Is jealousy a sign of love? ❑ No ❑ Yes

6 Should your romantic partner intuitively know what you need? ❑ No ❑ Yes

7 If your relationship has a lot of conflict, would you end it? ❑ No ❑ Yes

8 If the passion goes out of your relationship, would you:
  a) end the relationship.
  b) accept it and stay committed to the relationship. Passion will come and go.
  c) insist that you both get therapy.

9 Do you expect you and your partner to be monogamous? ❑ No ❑ Yes

10 If your spouse cheated on you, would you
   a) leave him/her
   b) see a counselor and work on the relationship
   c) get even and have an affair too.
   d) not worry about it; having an affair isn't a big deal.

11 Do you eventually want children? ❏ No ❏ Yes

12 Is it a good idea to put children in daycare from ages 1 to 5? ❏ No ❏ Yes
Why or why not? _____

13 If your potential or actual spouse doesn't want children, and you do (or vice versa) would you break up the relationship over this issue? ❏ No ❏ Yes

14 Should couples have relationship training before they get married? ❏ No ❏ Yes

Now read the following text. You will re-examine this survey later.

Myths about Marriage

READING 7.1

Marriage Myths

by Daniel Wayne Matthews

1. Marriage is still the prominent partnered relationship in the American culture as evidenced by the 2.3 million marriages recorded in 1992. This holds true despite the high number of divorces and the negative stereotypes of marriage portrayed in movies and on television. Although one of every two new marriages ends in divorce, many couples sincerely vow to remain in their marriage "til death do us part."

2. A number of stumbling blocks inevitably arise to challenge the couple's best intentions. For example, young couples often fail to see things realistically. Caught up in the romance and in the excitement of wedding plans, many couples are unable to envision what their relationship will be like on a routine, day-to-day basis. For those anticipating a Cinderella-like happily-ever-after storybook marriage year after year, disappointment is likely to come sooner or later. Conflict, crises, and daily hassles are part of virtually every marriage relationship.

3. Discussing important issues like money, children, role expectations, sex, and in-laws before marriage will help set the stage for a smoother relationship.

Realistic Expectations

4 Many, if not most, expectations for marriage are based on idealized myths. If realities within a relationship do not match the myth, one or both partners may think they have made a terrible mistake. A few of the myths about marriage are:

5 **Myth:** *A good marriage will always be romantic.*

6 **Reality:** Virtually all relationships experience peaks and valleys. Sometimes, the realities of married life will often cloud over romantic feelings. Scott Peck, in his book *The Road Less Traveled*, stated –"Every couple falls in love; every couple falls out of love." Just because the *feelings of love* are not always present doesn't necessarily mean a lack of love; love is more of a choice than a feeling.

7 **Myth:** *Marriage will make me happy.*

8 **Reality:** A marriage partner does not have the power or ability to *make* another person happy. A person's sense of happiness must come from deep inside himself. Relationship in marriage has the potential of complementing individual happiness and well-being, but it cannot be the primary source.

9 **Myth:** *If we really love each other, everything else will fall into place.*

10 **Reality:** Marriage needs constant nurturing. Because of individual, societal, and environmental changes, marriage is always in a state of flux; it is a dynamic relationship rather than a static one. Constant sensitivity to one another's needs and continual adaptation to relational changes are necessary to keep love alive.

11 **Myth:** *My partner should intuitively know my needs.*

12 **Reality:** Regardless of a spouse's intelligence or personal strengths, she does not have the ability to read her partner's mind. Needs for security, affection, emotional support, encouragement, or physical assistance often must be verbalized in clear language, sometimes repeatedly. If the need is something the spouse can realistically provide, she must first know the need exists.

13 **Myth:** *Conflict means a lack of love.*

14 **Reality:** Conflict is inevitable, but it doesn't have to be damaging to the marriage relationship. Partners have different viewpoints and different feelings based on their background and previous experiences. Those differences do not mean that one partner is right and the other wrong; it just means they are not alike in their thoughts or feelings. Conflict, when dealt with appropriately, can be healthy for a relationship in that new ideas and new ways of looking at things are introduced to each partner and to the relationship.

15 Both you and your spouse will enter marriage with a set of expectations, some of which will be quite different from the other's. You may expect that the romance will never fade in your relationship; your spouse may not be naturally romantic. Each of you have expectations regarding various roles you will play in the marriage. The woman may expect that she will have a career, and the household chores will be shared equally between herself and her husband. The man, however, may be somewhat traditional and may see cooking and cleaning as his wife's responsibility. Role expectations are not as

clear cut in the 1990's as they once were. Each couple would be wise to communicate honestly about marital expectations before the wedding takes place.

16 Couples who take the time and effort to educate themselves about quality relationships and who practice effective communication skills in their interactions with each other have a greater likelihood of experiencing a satisfying, fulfilling relationship together for many years.

COMPREHENSION

1 What introduction style does Matthews use?
 a) anecdote
 b) historical background
 c) general background
 d) opposite view

2 What is Matthew's main point? Find a sentence from the text that sums up the main idea.

_____

_____

3 Briefly summarize Matthew's responses to the following myths.

a) A good marriage will always be romantic.
 It's not true. Romance comes and goes, but it doesn't mean there is no love.

b) Marriage will make me happy. _____

_____

c) If we really love each other, everything else will fall into place. _____

_____

d) My partner should intuitively know my needs. _____

_____

e) Conflict means a lack of love. _____

_____

4 How do your answers to the "Relationship Survey" compare to the points in Matthew's article. Do you believe in many of the marriage myths? How realistic are your expectations about marriage/commitment?

_____

_____

_____

_____

Love

5 In your opinion, why do so many marriages end in divorce?

_____

_____

_____

LISTENING: Love

LISTENING COMPREHENSION

Love is in the air. Poems have been written about it. Songs have been sung about it. But what is love? Listen to two very contradictory views on the subject.

Listen and take notes. Then complete the chart below.

	ALISON MCKENDRY	MARTIN PLOUGHMAN
What is love?		(Compare infatuation with love)
Love vs. friendship		
Are humans monogamous?		

Chapter 7

	ALISON MCKENDRY	MARTIN PLOUGHMAN
Opinion about marriage		
Advice		

DISCUSSION

1 Which person do you agree with? What is love?

2 Can friendship turn into love?

Reading Tip: Making Inferences

Sometimes the main idea of a text is not stated directly. On those occasions, you must infer what the author means to say. *Infer* means to look for clues and then to make a deduction.[1]

For example, read the following paragraph. The author doesn't directly state his opinion. Try to infer the author's meaning.

> The band cost about $2500 for the night. We didn't go high-class: we just found competent musicians. The hall rented for $800 that night, and we figured we got a good deal. We had to decorate it ourselves. There were flowers on every table (twenty-five dollars each bouquet), rented china and silverware ($850), tablecloths, tables and chairs ($300). The catered food worked out to be $30 per person, multiplied by three hundred. Well, you can imagine. And of course there is the alcohol: we spent over $11,000. This is not counting the dresses, the tuxedos, the photographer, the rented limos. Sure, it was a "special night." Too bad the guests of honour split up three months later.

1. Note: *Infer* is often confused with the word *imply*. Only a speaker or writer may *imply* something, for this word means "to suggest without stating." The listener or reader may *infer* an idea from what was said or written, since this verb means "to conclude from reasoning."

To answer the following questions you must make inferences.

1 What is the subject of this text?

_____

2 What is the author's relationship to the guests of honour?

_____

3 What is the author's main point?

_____

_____

Now read the following text.

> Sure, marriage is a great thing. We all grew up with that image of the beautiful bride in her wedding gown and the groom with his tuxedo and slick hair. There is the flower girl who tosses rose petals, and the organ music…
>
> Except that some of us cannot get legally married in North America. People say that it is against "family values" for us to get married. Some people even call my relationship with my partner "aberrant."
>
> Hey, I'm not complaining: when I look at the rest of you and note that over 50% of you get divorced, I realize that the institution of marriage is not something that I will necessarily miss. On the other hand, I'd like a ritual that would show my partner how I feel. I'd also like the same legal privileges that married people have. It's not such a bizarre idea. The Netherlands has done it. *The Washington Post* reports that the 190-33 vote in the Dutch lower house marks the latest instance of the Netherlands breaking social-policy barriers.
>
> When is it going to be my time? When is that little statue on the top of the wedding cake going to reflect my reality?

To answer the following questions you must make inferences.

1 Why can't the author get married?

_____

2 What is the author's main point?

_____

3 What clues helped you infer what this text is about?

_____

_____

_____

READING 7.2

In the following text, noted science fiction author John Collier writes about the nature of love. To appreciate this text, you must imagine that the impossible is possible.

The Chaser

John Collier (1901-1980)

1. Alan Austen, as nervous as a kitten, went up certain dark and creaky stairs in the neighborhood of Pell Street, and peered about for a long time on the dim landing before he found the name he wanted written obscurely on one of the doors.

2. He pushed open this door, as he had been told to do, and found himself in a tiny room, which contained no furniture but a plain kitchen table, a rocking-chair, and an ordinary chair. On one of the dirty buff-colored walls were a couple of shelves, containing in all perhaps a dozen bottles and jars.

3. An old man sat in the rocking-chair, reading a newspaper. Alan, without a word, handed him the card he had been given. "Sit down, Mr. Austen," said the old man very politely. "I am glad to make your acquaintance."

4. "Is it true," asked Alan, "that you have a certain mixture that has – er – quite extraordinary effects?"

5. "My dear sir," replied the old man, "my stock in trade is not very large – I don't deal in laxatives and teething mixtures – but such as it is, it is varied. I think nothing I sell has effects which could be precisely described as ordinary."

6. "Well, the fact is…" began Alan.

7. "Here, for example," interrupted the old man, reaching for a bottle from the shelf. "Here is a liquid as colourless as water, almost tasteless, quite imperceptible in coffee, wine, or any other beverage. It is also quite imperceptible to any known method of autopsy."

8. "Do you mean it is a poison?" cried Alan, very much horrified.

9. "Call it a glove-cleaner if you like," said the old man indifferently. "Maybe it will clean gloves. I have never tried. One might call it a life-cleaner. Lives need cleaning sometimes."

10. "I want nothing of that sort," said Alan.

11. "Probably it is just as well," said the old man. "Do you know the price of this? For one teaspoonful, which is sufficient, I ask five thousand dollars. Never less. Not a penny less."

12. "I hope all your mixtures are not as expensive," said Alan apprehensively.

13. "Oh dear, no," said the old man. "It would be no good charging that sort of price for a love potion, for example. Young people who need a love potion very seldom have five thousand dollars. Otherwise they would not need a love potion."

14. "I am glad to hear that," said Alan.

15. "I look at it like this," said the old man. "Please a customer with one article, and he will come back when he needs another. Even if it is more costly. He will save up for it, if necessary."

16 "So," said Alan, "you really do sell love potions?"

17 "If I did not sell love potions," said the old man, reaching for another bottle, "I should not have mentioned the other matter to you. It is only when one is in a position to oblige that one can afford to be so confidential."

18 "And these potions," said Alan. "They are not just – just – er –"

19 "Oh, no," said the old man. "Their effects are permanent, and extend far beyond the mere casual impulse. But they include it. Oh, yes they include it. Bountifully, insistently. Everlastingly."

20 "Dear me!" said Alan, attempting a look of scientific detachment. "How very interesting!"

21 "But consider the spiritual side," said the old man.

22 "I do, indeed," said Alan.

23 "For indifference," said the old man, "they substitute devotion. For scorn, adoration. Give one tiny measure of this to the young lady – its flavor is imperceptible in orange juice, soup, or cocktails – and however gay and giddy she is, she will change altogether. She will want nothing but solitude and you."

24 "I can hardly believe it," said Alan. "She is so fond of parties."

25 "She will not like them any more," said the old man. "She will be afraid of the pretty girls you may meet."

26 "She will actually be jealous?" cried Alan in a rapture. "Of me?"

27 "Yes, she will want to be everything to you."

28 "She is, already. Only she doesn't care about it."

29 "She will, when she has taken this. She will care intensely. You will be her sole interest in life."

30 "Wonderful!" cried Alan.

31 "She will want to know all you do," said the old man. "All that has happened to you during the day. Every word of it. She will want to know what you are thinking about, why you smile suddenly, why you are looking sad."

32 "That is love!" cried Alan.

33 "Yes," said the old man. "How carefully she will look after you! She will never allow you to be tired, to sit in a **draught**, to neglect your food. If you are an hour late, she will be terrified. She will think you are killed, or that some **siren** has caught you."

34 "I can hardly imagine Diana like that!" cried Alan, overwhelmed with joy.

35 "You will not have to use your imagination," said the old man. "And, by the way, since there are always sirens, if by any chance you should, later on, slip a little, you need not worry. She will forgive you, in the end. She will be terribly hurt, of course, but she will forgive you – in the end."

36 "That will not happen," said Alan fervently.

draught air that blows into a room

siren beautiful, tempting woman

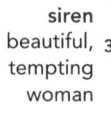

Chapter 7

37 "Of course not," said the old man. "But, if it did, you need not worry. She would never divorce you. Oh, no! And, of course, she will never give you the least, the very least, grounds for – uneasiness."

38 "And how much," said Alan, "is this wonderful mixture?"

dear
expensive
(British term)

39 "It is not as **dear**," said the old man, "as the glove-cleaner, or life-cleaner, as I sometimes call it. No. That is five thousand dollars, never a penny less. One has to be older than you are, to indulge in that sort of thing. One has to save up for it."

40 "But the love potion?" said Alan.

41 "Oh, that," said the old man, opening the drawer in the kitchen table, and taking out a tiny, rather dirty-looking phial. "That is just a dollar."

42 "I can't tell you how grateful I am," said Alan, watching him fill it.

43 "I like to oblige," said the old man. "Then customers come back, later in life, when they are better off, and want more expensive things. Here you are. You will find it very effective."

44 "Thank you again," said Alan. "Good-bye."

45 "Au revoir," said the man.

VOCABULARY

Using Context Clues

Read how the following terms are used in context. Then, write down the part of speech of each term: Is the term an adjective, noun, or verb? Next, without using your dictionary, guess the meaning of the terms.

	Part of Speech	Definition
1 creaky (1)		
2 peered (1)		
3 dim (1)		
4 landing (1)		

COMPREHENSION

1 Who is the old man? Is his business legitimate? (What are some clues about the type of business he has?)

2 Although the text doesn't directly describe Alan, what can you infer about his personality? What type of person is he?

_____
_____

3 What is Diana like? Look for clues in the text and describe Diana.

_____
_____

4 What six distinct qualities will the love potion give Diana? Identify the quality and the paragraph number. Include a short quotation.

FOR EXAMPLE: *She will change from an outgoing person to a solitary one: "She will want nothing but solitude and you" (23).*

_____
_____
_____
_____
_____
_____
_____
_____

5 Why is the old man probably selling the love potion for such a low price? Make a guess.

_____
_____

6 What could a "life cleaner" be?

_____
_____

7 What is the message of the text? (Note: the message is not directly stated. Try to infer what the author's message is.)

_____
_____

DISCUSSION / WRITTEN RESPONSE

Describe what Paul feels for Diana. Is it love? Is it infatuation? Is it something else?

Reading Tip:
Think about the Theme (meaning)

Plot tells us what happens in a story. Character tells us about the people in a story. Theme tells us *the underlying meaning in a story*. The theme is a statement that provides insight into human existence. Themes are universal ideas.

Most authors do not tell you explicitly what their story means. Instead, the situations that occur and the reactions of the characters allow the reader to discover what the central meaning (or theme) of the story is.

Making a statement of theme

- Theme must be expressed in the form of a complete statement.

    For example, one of the subjects of "Next Door" by Kurt Vonnegut is "lost innocence." However, that is not a statement of theme. To express this idea in a statement you could write: *"Next Door" illustrates that parents cannot stop children from losing their innocence.*

- The statement of theme must express a universal truth.

    Don't make narrow, specific statements of theme. For example, a student suggested that the theme of "Next Door" is "Never trust people." But is this really a universal truth? If so, the world would be a very sad place indeed. Remember that your statement of theme must be generally true.

Some stories may have more than one theme. Several different statements of theme may be correct. Most importantly, you must be able to support your statement of theme by referring to elements in the story.

Look at the following elements of the story before you make your statement of theme.

a) The title: After you have read the story, does the title now have a deeper significance?
b) The central events: Does the plot illustrate a universal truth?
c) The main character: Does the main character evolve and develop a new understanding about life?

Now write a statement of theme about one or more of the following texts.

"The Greatest Player" (Chapter 3)

_____

_____

"Conscience" (Chapter 4)

_____

_____

"Next Door" (Chapter 5)

"Bernice Bobs Her Hair" (Chapter 6)

"The Chaser" (Chapter 7)

Essay Topics

Write an essay about one of the following topics. Your essay should have an appealing introduction and a short conclusion.

1. There are three mistakes that people in love make. (You could quote from the text "The Chaser.")
2. Marriage for life is (or is not) realistic.
3. Couples should (or should not) stay together for the sake of the children.
4. Marriage is an out-dated institution.

You can read more classic short stories at the following site.
www.online-library.org/fictions/

Find out about the history of marriage at the following site.
marriage.about.com/mlibrary.htm

APPENDIX 1 How to Do Oral Presentations

There are a few points to remember when you make an oral presentation.

PLAN YOUR PRESENTATION

- Structure your presentation. Include an appealing introduction. Use facts or examples to support your main points. Remember to conclude your presentation.
- Write your presentation on cue cards. However, only write down key words and phrases. If you write your entire presentation on cue cards, you could end up getting confused and losing your place.
- Rehearse! Do not expect to ad-lib a formal presentation. Your teacher will not be impressed if you must frequently pause to think of something to say.
- Don't memorize your presentation or you'll sound too unnatural. It is better to speak to the audience and occasionally refer to your notes than to rattle off a memorized text.
- Time yourself. Before you give your report, ensure that your oral presentation respects the time limit your teacher has given you.

GIVE YOUR PRESENTATION

- Look at your audience. Don't look only at the teacher.
- Use notes to guide yourself through the presentation. Don't read.
- Use formal language. Don't say, *stuff*, *it sucks*, etc.
- When the assignment requires it, bring in visual or audio supports. This can make your presentation more interesting.

2 Speaking Presentation Topic – Classic Movie Analysis

PREPARATION

1) With a team of about four or five students, choose one of the following themes:

Ambition	History (fact vs. fiction)	Racism
Adolescence	Innocence Lost	The Supernatural
Heroism	Love	Travel

Each team member must find a film about that theme. Try to find films that were made in different time periods or find films that are in different genres (war / drama / comedy / science fiction / musical). Make sure that no one else in your team chooses the same film. Remember, it is boring for other students if you talk about a popular film that they have already seen.

2) Prepare your movie analysis *alone*. You should not share any information with your team members. They will be surprised on the day of your presentation.

HOW TO DO YOUR MOVIE ANALYSIS

Your analysis should have the following elements:

1. **Make an interesting introduction.** You could describe a scene, give background or historical information, or you could tell a story about when you first saw the film. Make your introduction interesting. End your introduction by stating your opinion of the film.

2. ***Briefly* describe what the story is about.** Don't give away surprise endings.

   Your description should be no more than about six sentences in length. Just describe the main elements of the plot. For example, *The Matrix* has a complicated plot that can be summed up in six sentences:

   > The basic premise of *The Matrix* is that the entire human race has been kept under control by Artificial Intelligence machines. The machines fool humans into believing that their everyday world is real when it is really just a dream. This "dream" world

is called the Matrix. A man called Morpheus was unplugged from the artificial system. With a team of five other people, he tries to free the human race. He believes that a young man named Neo can help him achieve this task.

The point is, make a <u>short</u> film summary!

3. **Describe the film's characters.**

   For this section of your analysis, you can go into more detail. Ask yourself the following questions about the central character(s).
   - How does the central character behave at the beginning of the film?
   - What are the central character's values? Ambitions? Hopes? Fears?
   - Does the central character change?
   - How important are the characters? Are they the most interesting part of the movie? (for example: *Forrest Gump* is a "character-driven" film.)

4. **Briefly describe the film's setting.**

   Look at the time, place, and culture. If you are describing a contemporary film, you could mention the appearance of the place, the predominant culture (conservative, rebellious, etc.), and the values (love, money, etc.)

   If you are reviewing an older film or if your film is about a past era, you could describe how life was different then. (Think about the family relationships, beliefs, music, social life, fashion, etc.)

5. **Conclusion.**

   How does this movie illustrate your team's theme? Describe the film's message. What lesson does the movie teach us? What does the movie tell us about human nature? Is the lesson convincing?

   Give the film a rating out of ten. Make a suggestion to your classmates.

POINTS TO REMEMBER

- Keep the language formal. If you do not like the film, don't say, "It sucks." It would be better to say something like, "The film was unsatisfying."
- Show your audience a 1- to 2-minute video clip. Find a scene that is particularly fascinating (or if you hated the film, find a scene that is really bad).
- Show your video clip at a relevant point during your presentation. For example, if your clip illustrates the interesting characters, then show it when you discuss the characters.

Your teacher will suggest a length for your presentation. Practice your presentation and time yourself to make sure that you respect that length.

CLASSIC FILM WEBSITES

A classic films site: www.moderntimes.com/palace/welcome.htm
A movie lover's paradise: movies.go.com
This site gives brief plot descriptions of 100 great films: www.filmsite.org/momentsindx.html

APPENDIX 3 Classic Movies

Here are some classic movie suggestions. You don't have to choose a movie from this list.

DRAMAS

Gone With The Wind (1939)
The Philadelphia Story (1940)
The Maltese Falcon (1941)
Citizen Kane (1941)
Casablanca (1942)
It's a Wonderful Life (1946)
All About Eve (1950)
Sunset Boulevard (1950)
A Streetcar Named Desire (1951)
On the Waterfront (1954)
Rebel Without a Cause (1955)
East of Eden (1955)
Lust for Life (1956)
Vertigo (1958) or any Alfred Hitchcock film
Lolita (1961)
The Misfits (1961)
To Kill a Mockingbird (1962)
Dr. Zhivago (1965)
Bonnie and Clyde (1967)
Guess Who's Coming to Dinner (1967)
Midnight Cowboy (1969)
Butch Cassidy and the Sundance Kid (1969)
The Graduate (1967)
The Godfather (1972)
The Sting (1973)
Rocky (1976)
Taxi Driver (1976)
Being There (1979)
The Elephant Man (1980)
Gandhi (1982)
Stand By Me (1986)
Dead Poet's Society (1989)
Do the Right Thing (1989)
Goodfellas (1990)
The Crying Game (1992)
Forrest Gump (1994)
Pulp Fiction (1994)
Fargo (1996)
Shine (1996)
Billy Elliot (2000)

COMEDIES

City Lights, Modern Times, or any Charlie Chaplin film (1930s)
Duck Soup (1933) or any Marx Brothers Film
Some Like It Hot (1959)
The Apartment (1960)
Dr. Strangelove (1964)
The Pink Panther (1964)
The Odd Couple (1968)
M.A.S.H. (1970)
Blazing Saddles (1974)
One Flew Over the Cuckoo's Nest (1975)
Annie Hall (1977)
Tootsie (1982)
Zelig (1983)
Ghostbusters (1985)
When Harry Met Sally (1989)
My Cousin Vinny (1992)
The Player (1992)
The Full Monty (1997)
There's Something About Mary (1997)
The Waterboy (1998)
Man on the Moon (2000)

MUSICALS / MUSICAL DRAMAS

The Wizard of Oz (1939)
Fantasia (1940)
West Side Story (1961)
My Fair Lady (1964)
A Hard Day's Night (1964)
The Sound of Music (1965)
To Sir With Love (1967) (about racism)
Willy Wonka and the Chocolate Factory (1971)
Tommy (1972)
The Rocky Horror Picture Show (1975)
Grease (1977)
Amadeus (1984)
The Commitments (1992)
Oh Brother, Where Art Thou (2001)
Moulin Rouge (2001)
Chicago (2002)

SCIENCE FICTION / FANTASY

Metropolis (1926)
Day of the Triffids (1962)
Planet of the Apes (1967)
A Clockwork Orange (1971) or any Stanley Kubrick film
The Exorcist (1973)
Star Wars (1977)
Blade Runner (1982)
The Matrix (1998)
The Blair Witch Project (1999)
The Sixth Sense (2000)
Signs (2002)
Lord of the Rings (2002)
Harry Potter (2002)

WAR / BATTLES

Battleship Potemkin (1925)
Paths of Glory (1957)
Ben Hur (1959)
Apocalypse Now (1971)
The Deer Hunter (1978)
Platoon (1986)
Schindler's List (1993)
The Thin Red Line (1998)
Saving Private Ryan (1998)

SOME CLASSIC MOVIE SUGGESTIONS (by theme)

AMBITION
- Citizen Kane (1941)
- The Godfather (1972)
- Goodfellas (1990)
- Fargo (1996)
- Forrest Gump (1994)
- Apocalypse Now (1971)
- The Graduate (1967)
- Butch Cassidy and Sundance Kid (1969)
- Billy Elliot (2000)
- The Full Monty (1997)
- Tootsie (1982)
- The Sting (1973)
- Rocky (1976)
- Taxi Driver (1976)
- My Fair Lady (1964)

ADOLESCENCE
- American Pie (1999)
- Billy Elliot (2000)
- Rebel Without a Cause (1955)
- West Side Story (1961)
- To Sir With Love (1967)
- Stand By Me (1986)
- A Clockwork Orange (1971)
- Grease (1977)
- Heathers (1989)
- Sid and Nancy (1986)
- St. Elmo's Fire (1985)
- The Commitments (1992)
- Lolita (1961)
- Ghost World (2001)
- Lost and Delirious (2001)

HEROISM
- Paths of Glory (1957)
- Ben Hur (1959)
- Schindler's List (1993)
- The Sound of Music (1965)
- Gandhi (1982)
- Apollo 13 (1995)
- Born on the 4th of July (1989)
- Shine (1996)
- Amistad (1997)
- Elephant Man (1980)
- Gandhi (1982)
- Unbreakable (2000)
- Erin Brockovitch (2000)
- Elizabeth (1998)
- Any James Bond movie

HISTORY: FACT VS. FICTION
- Elizabeth (1998)
- Citizen Kane (1941)
- Gandhi (1982)
- Bonnie and Clyde (1967)
- Titanic (1998)
- Thirteen Days (2001)
- JFK (1991)
- Amistad (1997)
- Schindler's List (1993)
- Saving Private Ryan (1998)
- Sunset Boulevard (1950)
- Hurricane (2000)
- Braveheart (1995)
- The Great Escape (1963)
- Quills (2000)

INNOCENCE LOST
- Lolita (1961)
- Shine (1996)
- Billy Elliot (2000)
- The Graduate (1967)
- Apocalypse Now (1971)
- The Exorcist (1973)
- The Misfits (1961)
- Dead Poet's Society (1989)
- The Player (1992)
- Summer of '42 (1971)
- The Godfather (1972)
- Taxi Driver (1976)
- Good Will Hunting (1997)
- Stand By Me (1986)
- A Clockwork Orange (1971)

LOVE
- Almost any Charlie Chaplin film
- A Streetcar Named Desire (1951)
- The Crying Game (1992)
- The Graduate (1971)
- Romeo and Juliet (1968)
- Play Misty for Me (1971)
- Annie Hall (1977)
- When Harry Met Sally (1989)
- Titanic (1998)
- Casablanca (1942)
- The Bridges of Madison County (1995)
- Gone With the Wind (1939)
- The Sound of Music (1965)
- Breakfast at Tiffany's (1961)
- Fatal Attraction (1987)

PREJUDICE
- Little Big Man (1970)
- Guess Who's Coming to Dinner (1965)
- Gandhi (1982)
- No Way Out (1950)
- Dances With Wolves (1990)
- One Flew Over the Cuckoo's Nest (1975)
- Amistad (1997)
- Malcolm X (1992)
- Remember the Titans (2000)
- Boys Don't Cry (1999)
- Snow Falling on Cedars (2000)
- Schindler's List (1993)
- Rain Man (1988)
- To Sir With Love (1967)
- A Clockwork Orange (1971)

SUPERNATURAL
- The Sixth Sense (2000)
- The X-Files (1998)
- The Exorcist (1973)
- Ghost (1990)
- Unbreakable (2001)
- The Gift (2001)
- Any Dracula movie
- ET (1982)
- Poltergeist (1982)
- It's a Wonderful Life (1946)
- The Picture of Dorian Gray (1945)
- Time Bandits (1981)
- King Kong (1933)
- Signs (2002)
- Lord of the Rings (2002)
- Harry Potter (2002)

TRAVEL / SELF DISCOVERY
- Castaway (2000)
- Thelma and Louise (1991)
- Dr. Zhivago (1965)
- Bonnie and Clyde (1967)
- Blade Runner (1982)
- Rain Man (1988)
- My Fair Lady (1964)
- The Wizard of Oz (1939)
- On the Waterfront (1954)
- It's a Wonderful Life (1946)
- Desperately Seeking Susan (1985)
- Midnight Cowboy (1969)
- Stranger than Paradise (1984), Down By Law (1986), or any Jim Jarmusch film
- Oh Brother, Where Art Thou (2001)

APPENDIX 4
Twenty Controversial Issues

These issues can be used in oral or written presentations or with debates.

1. **Violent Parents at Sporting Events:** What should be done about violent parents at kids' sporting events?

2. **Spanking:** In a recent case, Justice David McCombs (Ontario Superior Court) upheld the right of parents and teachers to use "reasonable force" to discipline children without fear of being dragged into court for child abuse. Should spanking be illegal?

3. **Thin Models Banished:** British magazine owners have agreed to a voluntary code to banish ultra-thin models from their magazines. Canadian magazine owners refuse to follow Britain's lead, arguing that "we hate to label all models as anorexic. Some women are naturally thin."

4. **Kids Face Adult Charges:** When a 12- or 13-year-old commits murder, should that child face adult charges? Why or why not?

5. **Assistance for Tobacco Victims:** In a landmark class-action U.S. lawsuit, people suffering from tobacco-related illnesses were awarded $145 billion. The tobacco companies have lost several lawsuits to date, but so far have not paid one cent. Should tobacco companies be held liable for misleading the public about the dangerous properties of tobacco?

6. **Mercy Killing:** A Saskatchewan farmer, Robert Latimer, was convicted for ending the life of his daughter Tracy. In October 1993, he put his severely disabled daughter into his pickup truck and then piped exhaust fumes into the cab of the truck. What should happen to family members in cases like this?

7. **Sex Lives of Politicians:** John F. Kennedy had affairs that were not reported to the media. Bill Clinton's affairs were highly publicized. Should a politician's sex life be reported by the media? Some argue that voters should have the right to know about the morals and values of their leaders; others argue that this information is none of our business. Where do you stand on the issue?

8. **Affirmative Action Hiring Policies:** Many jobs, placements in schools, and other places in society have been reserved for women or visible minorities; the purpose is to redress a historical imbalance. Is this fair? Why or why not?

9. **Gun Lawsuits:** Should gun-makers be held liable for what is done with their products?

10. **Gun Controls:** How useful are gun control measures? Do gun controls infringe on the rights of hunters and gun collectors?

11. **Gay Rights:** Should gay couples have the right to legally marry and to adopt children?

12. **Television:** Does television have a positive or negative impact on our culture? Should children have limited TV-watching time?

13. **Sex in Movies:**

    a) Is the movie rating system redundant? Now that kids can rent videos and watch R- or X-rated movies at home, should the whole ratings system just be scrapped?

    b) Do current movies (e.g., *Scary Movie*, *American Pie*, etc.) contain too much sex for their often pre-teen audiences? Is sex overemphasized in films?

14. **The Death Penalty:** The United States has it. Canada, Britain, and most of the world's nations don't. Where do you stand on the issue of the death penalty?

15. **Government in the Gambling Industry:** Are government-owned casinos and video gambling terminals good or bad for the population?

16. **Ritalin and ADD:** Some medical practitioners argue that Attention Deficit Disorder is an "invented" disease that was created to sell pharmaceutical products. What do you think?

17. **Women's Equality:** In North America, have women finally attained equal status with men? Think about the following areas: politics, childcare, or the workplace.

18. **Female Teachers with Male Students:** Both the United States and Canada have dealt with high-profile cases of female teachers having intimate relationships with their teenaged students. Should female teachers be treated exactly the same way as male teachers who become involved with female students?

19. **Childcare:** Is it a good or bad idea to send small children to daycares for the first years of their lives?

20. **Global Warming:** How serious is it? What should governments do about it?